IMAGES
of America

SHEPPARD AIR FORCE BASE

On the Cover: These flight-line service technicians are standing on a boarding ramp with "Welcome to Sheppard A.F.B." imprinted on the side. This photograph is dated March 13, 1952. (Courtesy of Sheppard Air Force Base.)

IMAGES
of America

SHEPPARD AIR FORCE BASE

SMSGT Norman Wayne Brown, USAF, Retired
Foreword by pioneer aviator Jim Foreman

ARCADIA PUBLISHING

ISBN 978-1-4671-3464-4

Published by Arcadia Publishing
Charleston, South Carolina

Printed in the United States of America

Library of Congress Control Number: 2015941079

For all general information, please contact Arcadia Publishing:
Telephone 843-853-2070
Fax 843-853-0044
E-mail sales@arcadiapublishing.com
For customer service and orders:
Toll-Free 1-888-313-2665

Visit us on the Internet at www.arcadiapublishing.com

To my wife, Bettie, for her support and assistance; to the memory of my son Jason Wayne Brown; and finally, to all the men and women of the armed forces who make the sacrifices to keep our country free

Contents

Foreword 6

Acknowledgments 7

Introduction 8

1. World War I Pilot Training 9
2. Museum of North Texas 27
3. Military Postcards and Posters 41
4. Birth of Sheppard Field 55
5. Female Pilots of World War II 69
6. Sheppard Becomes an Air Force 85
7. Sheppard Today 109

FOREWORD

Norman Wayne Brown is a tireless researcher when tracing the history of someone or some place, as witnessed by the scope of his books on *Early Settlers of the Panhandle Plains*, by Arcadia Publishing; coauthor of *A Lawless Breed, John Wesley Hardin, Texas Reconstruction, and Violence in the Wild West* by the University of North Texas Press; and *Life on the Texas Frontier*, edited and published by Norman. He has also written numerous articles about the Old West for national magazines and a Western scholarly journal and is a public speaker in great demand. Norman came across a number of photographs of wrecked airplanes. The only thing on any of them was the date: 1917. With the photographs was a newspaper clipping telling of the crashes of four airplanes in two days in the small town of Crowell, Texas. What added to the mystery was three of the airplanes had Canadian Air Corps markings, traced to Call Field in Wichita Falls, Texas, which was one of the first Army pilot-training fields during World War I. Before that, all training was conducted in Canada but moved to Texas where weather and flying conditions were much better.

Call Field was the impetus for the military establishing Sheppard Field when World War II came along and reestablished as Sheppard Air Force Base after the war. Norman spent the last six years of his military career assigned to Sheppard, so he comes highly qualified to provide a great book on Sheppard Air Force Base.

—Jim Foreman

Note: Jim Foreman began flying at 16, earned both private and commercial licenses, and ferried all types of military surplus airplanes. He was a crop duster in California. Jim built a replica of a 1915 German Fokker and flew in air shows and movies. He is the author of numerous books with *The Flight of the Temporal Cub* and a book about his experiences during the Korean War titled *SCARWAF*.

Acknowledgments

I am grateful to Sarah Bellian for locating photographs of Call Field. I would like to thank Lita Watson of the Wichita County Archives and Charles Campbell, director of the Museum of North Texas, Wichita Falls, Texas. Also, a thank-you is owed to Jim Foreman, whose knowledge of aviation was of great assistance in the identification of many images. And a special acknowledgment to Bill Steward, who can see the lights of Sheppard Air Force Base from his front porch; Bill is also a local historian. There are many others who provided assistance in this project, and the list would be too long to mention everyone, but to those who helped, you have my sincere thanks.

Images in this catalogue come from a large variety of sources, including the Scurry County Museum, the US Air Force, the Museum of North Texas, the Wichita County Archives, and the collections of L.L. Kaylor and Carl McKinnon.

INTRODUCTION

Time has erased all signs of Call Field, an Army air field established in 1917 near the city of Wichita Falls, Texas. The only evidence is a marker and a couple of World War I aerial photographers' collections donated to the Museum of North Texas in downtown Wichita Falls. Little has been written about the brave young men who wanted to earn their wings and become pilots. When the First World War ended, the Army closed the field and nature reclaimed all 46 buildings, including the barracks, hangers, and the hospital building. Five hundred flyers received their wings there, and the 34 men who died during training were shipped back to their hometowns for burial. Call Field was almost forgotten.

In 1929, Ms. Edith McKanna, born and raised on her family ranch in Scurry County, Texas, became the first female pilot in the state of Texas and also the first female in Texas to own her own plane. When World War II came, she donated her plane to the war effort. She was a captain in the Civil Air Patrol and liaison with the Army Air Corps. At nearby Avenger Field in Sweetwater, Texas, other females were being trained to fly military aircraft. They not only ferried airplanes but flew as test pilots and did target towing for gunnery practice. They were considered expendable. It is an honor to include those brave young ladies within these pages.

Wichita Falls was dormant for military activity until World War II came. Three-hundred acres were donated for a token price of $1 by cattleman J.S. Bridwell, and a training facility was established and named Sheppard Field after US senator Morris E. Sheppard. All types of training took place, from basic to advanced pilot training, and reached a peak of over 46,000 troops. After the war ended, the military deactivated Sheppard on August 31, 1946, but before the dust settled the military reopened the field as Sheppard Air Force Base in August 1948.

The US Air Force has operated three training schools at Sheppard by providing training in aircraft maintenance and various specialties for units Air Force wide. The 82nd Training Wing has an impressive record as being the largest technical training unit in the Air Force and has graduated approximately 65,000 students each year for many years. The total number of people trained at the base since its beginning reaches into the millions.

One

World War I Pilot Training

Call Field, Wichita Falls, Texas. Call Field was established by the US Army as an ideal location for fair-weather flying as one of five locations in Texas for pilot training. Call Field faded into obscurity years ago, and today it is a "ghost army field." Sheppard Air Force Base may not have become reality without the World War I soldiers of Call Field paving the way. (Courtesy of Scurry County Museum.)

Lupton Lewis Kaylor. Pictured is Sfc. Lupton Lewis Kaylor, an aerial photographer assigned to Call Field. Kaylor's extensive photograph collection was donated to the Museum of North Texas in Wichita Falls, Texas. (L.L. Kaylor Collection.)

Call Field. Seen are some of the buildings and water tower at Call Field. Photographer Carl Lee McKinnon Jr. took this photograph from the roof of a building. The town of Wichita Falls can be seen in the background. Corporal McKinnon was also an aerial photographer assigned to Call Field in Sergeant First Class Kaylor's unit. (Carl McKinnon Collection.)

CPL. CARL LEE MCKINNON. McKinnon poses here dressed for aerial flight with his leather jacket, ascot, cap, and headgear. Like all of the other photographers, McKinnon usually flew with instructors, thereby improving their chances of survival. McKinnon returned to the Wichita Falls area after the war. He was born on April 13, 1894, and died on November 13, 1991. (Carl McKinnon Collection.)

FATAL CRASH. Carl McKinnon was scheduled to be on the flight of this aircraft in 1917 but was replaced by Douglas McGuire. Both the pilot and McGuire were killed in the crash. The crash had a sobering effect on McKinnon, knowing he was saved by the hand of faith. (Carl McKinnon Collection.)

Jenny Taking Flight. Carl McKinnon took this photograph of pilot training at Call Field with this airplane taking off from the dirt runway. The airplane used for training at Call Field was the Curtiss JN-4D biplane, known as the "Jenny." A restored and fully operational Jenny is on display at the Museum of North Texas (see chapter 2). (Carl McKinnon Collection.)

Group Photograph. This US Army Air Corps aerial photographer company at Call Field had no lettered designation at first; it was known only as the 192nd Aero Squadron of the US Army. Soon, the squadron became Company B of the 192nd Aero Squadron. This came about due to the increase in training and personnel. Photographer McKinnon is the man in the center with the square-bottomed tie. (Carl McKinnon Collection.)

MAJ. JAMES R. ALFONTE. Maj. James R. Alfonte was commander of Call Field in 1918. Archived documents indicate that Alfonte made frequent visits to the Wichita Falls area after he transferred to another location. He became involved in oil leases around the city and came to check on his sideline business. Major Alfonte went on to become a general officer and served with distinction during World War II. (Carl McKinnon Collection.)

MAJ. CHESTER P. DORLAND. Maj. Chester P. Dorland was the officer in charge of all flight training at Call Field during World War I. Call Field had fewer accidents than any other pilot-training location. Of course, he probably did not publicize getting his automobile stuck in the melting snow and calling upon a local farmer to give him a pull. His outing put a damper on having fun that day. (Carl McKinnon Collection.)

Two Soldiers at Call Field during Prayer. These unidentified soldiers have their hats removed while in prayer. It seems their mascot, a dog, has bitten the dust in some type of accident. The enlisted men lived in tents, as noted in the background, while the officers and cadets lived in barracks as noted on the left (Company D). Rank always comes with extra privileges. (L.L. Kaylor Collection.)

Airplane Hangar. These airplanes are housed in one of the many hangars at Call Field. Note the height of the structures, which probably had something to do with proper ventilation. There were windows on the side panels and ceiling to provide natural lighting for aircraft mechanics. It is reported that only four of these World War I Jenny aircraft remain today. (L.L. Kaylor Collection.)

Two Planes Collide. There were many airplane crashes while training cadets during World War I. In this image, two planes have collided in midair and fallen or one landed on top of the other near Call Field. Regardless, serious injury or death of the aviators was likely. (L.L. Kaylor Collection.)

Crash and Burn. Aviators had no parachutes in the early days. The fate of the instructor pilot and cadet of this crash is unknown, but chances are they did not survive. The plane went down in flames and crashed on the prairie while on a flight away from Call Field. The plane burned to the ground, scorching the earth. (L.L. Kaylor Collection.)

Airplanes in Flight. This image was taken of a squadron in flight. Call Field can be seen below during World War I pilot training at one of five airfields in Texas during 1917–1918. Photographer Kaylor took this photograph from his plane while the pilot soared above the other airplanes. (L.L. Kaylor Collection.)

Upside-Down Crash. This airplane crashed and flipped upside down on wide-open, level land on April 13, 1918; the date and tail number are imprinted on the image. The aircraft was probably repairable, and the aviators may or may not have been injured in this mishap. These crashes had to be photographed, and the images, along with accident reports, were sent to the upper echelon for review. (L.L. Kaylor Collection.)

CRASH INTO A FARMER'S FIELD. This training flight from Call Field on August 17, 1918, resulted in extensive damage to the front of tail no. 3885 after crash landing into a farmer's cotton field. The farmer most likely filed a claim for damages against the government. (L.L. Kaylor Collection.)

FORCED LANDING AND REPAIR. The instructor pilot and cadet from Call Field had to land in this field. The farmer's dog came out to greet them. The homing pigeon was released from the compartment behind the pilot's seat (see chapter 2) with a message to Call Field authorities reporting the mechanical problem, and two airplane mechanics were dispatched to try to repair the flying machine. (L.L. Kaylor Collection.)

Transit Hut Call Field. When Kaylor took this photograph at Call Field, he failed to provide any details of the event. The building appears to be a large Quonset hut providing temporary quarters for officers and enlisted men. The service ribbons on most of the uniforms indicate that this was likely debarkation quarters for soldiers being processed out and discharged at the end of World War I. (L.L. Kaylor Collection.)

Call Field Military Parade. This is a Call Field parade with a military brass band to commemorate the graduation of cadets who were receiving their wings as qualified aviators. According to Sergeant First Class Kaylor, this was the first photograph approved for release to the public. (L.L. Kaylor Collection.)

Soldier Shooting Bottles. This soldier was on a weekend pass, fishing and camping out. "Dead soldiers" was the title of the image and is a term used, even today, by many military personnel after emptying a bottle of whiskey, wine, or beer. When the bottle is standing up containing liquid, it signifies a live solider standing tall. When it is empty and laid on its side, it is dead, hence the term. This gentleman is about to shoot soldiers and kill the bottles as well as his automobile. (Scurry County Museum.)

Above Call Field. Pictured is an airplane in flight high above Call Field. The aerial photographer, Sfc. L.L. Kaylor, took the image from another airplane flying even higher while looking down at this flying machine. (L.L. Kaylor Collection.)

Pigpen Crash. This photograph shows an airplane that crashed into a pigpen. The solo flight went awry when the pilot flew too low and took off part of a barn roof and landed inside a pigpen in Crowell, Texas. The homing pigeon was released with a note to Call Field, and airplanes returned with repair parts, resulting in a total of four airplane crashes while trying to send replacement parts. (Scurry County Museum.)

A Crowd Gathering at Crash. The people of Crowell, Texas, like most citizens, had never seen an airplane, especially one up close and that had crashed to boot. For the residents, this event far exceeds anything they may have encountered at the county fair. It would be a story to tell their grandkids about. (Scurry County Museum.)

START IT UP, TROOPER! It appears that the pilot of this airplane had to set it down in a field as the weeds are in abundance. The landing may have been due to mechanical problems, but it was repaired and was then readied for flight. One man is ready to spin the prop after the pilot enters the cockpit. (Scurry County Museum.)

KAYLOR'S UNIT OF AERIAL PHOTOGRAPHERS. Kaylor was not in this photograph as he was the one who took the image. Corporal McKinnon is not in this group as he had departed Call Field for another assignment in Europe; Sfc. L.L. Kaylor would do the same very soon. (L.L. Kaylor Collection.)

SOLDIERS' BUNK SETUP. These soldiers are housed in a tent. One is reading a book, two are reading letters from home, and the soldier in the upper bunk has a homemade desktop and is writing a letter home. He has a bookcase behind his head, and he, like all soldiers, always had condiments to doctor the chow. (L.L. Kaylor Collection.)

ARMY AVIATORS. Soldiers with white bands on their hats were pilots. This large room provided mustering-out housing for this group of Army aviators who survived their own air war in Europe. They were the fortunate ones who were lucky to survive the Call Field training and even luckier to survive aerial combat. These airmen are ready to return to civilian life. Many were hooked on flying and went on to find some form of employment in the aircraft industry. (L.L. Kaylor Collection.)

CALL FIELD MESS HALL STAFF. Note the cook with a spoon in one hand ready to serve delicious gourmet chow to the troops while holding a furry feline in his left hand. Lieutenant Williams is the officer in charge of these gourmet chefs and has a cigarette ready for lighting. Surely, the cat was not shedding at the time of this photograph. (L.L. Kaylor Collection.)

Soldier Visits. Soldiers of World War I visited YMCAs. The Young Men's Christian Association was located near most Army bases during World War I in the United States and in Europe so that soldiers would have a faith-based place to visit while far away from hearth and home. (L.L. Kaylor Collection.)

First Plane Crash in Crowell, Texas. This is another view of the first airplane to crash in the town of Crowell, Texas (see page 20). The photograph shows exactly how much roof was taken from the barn's roof when the wheels of the airplane flew too low and crashed into the pigpen. (Scurry County Museum.)

Call Field Front Gate, Then and Now. The entrance to Call Field is pictured above during World War I. The sign reads, "Call Field Air Service, US Army, Entrance." The solider is carrying his rifle and dressed in an overcoat, which indicates it was taken during the winter of 1917 or 1918. The more recent photograph depicts houses in the area of the old gate. (Both, Museum of North Texas.)

FOUR AIRPLANE ACCIDENTS IN CROWELL

It seems that Crowell has come to be a dangerous place for the visits of airplanes. Four have either been wrecked or damaged within the last two weeks. The first one was almost a complete wreck after it struck the top of Frank Crews' house. It was shipped out on a flat car the next day.

The second one to be damaged was the first one coming after the accident of the wrecked machine. It struck a post at the M. L. Bird farm, breaking the propeller. The worst damage, however, was sustained by Bird himself when the enthusiastic youths crowded in to help repair the machine, and were not so particular as they might have been and tramped down a lot of his wheat. The next machine met a similar fate when it brought a propeller for the disabled plane when it was turned into a ditch to avoid running into a fence, the result of which was the loss of its own propeller. Repairs were brought and the machines were all apparently prepared to sail. When the last machine to leave started it never succeeded in making a good rise. While only a short distance above the telephone wires it yielded to the force of gravity and landed in L. I. Sanders' lot in the north part of town not more than three blocks from where it started.

The machine turned turtle, its tail making a graceful curve when it suddenly insisted on changing its course. It was lying flat of its back when the landing was affected while the aviators were trying to stand on their heads. Neither was hurt but the machine was considerably wrecked and had to be shipped out.

No explanation is given as to the cause of these accidents. There is no way of determining so far as we know. It may be bad gasoline, or bad atmosphere, or poor working condition of machines. Anyway, let us hope that Crowell is not to blame for them. We would like publicity, but not such as would likely cause aviators speak of us with a shudder.

NEWSPAPER CLIPPINGS. The newspaper clipping above gives the full details of four airplane crashes in Crowell, Texas. This was a time when carrier pigeons earned their birdseed by carrying messages from the pilots back to Call Field requesting help. The newspaper clipping below describes civilians Carl E. Thacker and Carl Wishon taking airplane rides with a pilot from Call Field. The article provides a hilarious account of a hair-raising event. (Both, Scurry County Museum.)

C. E. Thacker and Carl Wishon were taken for rides in the air ships Sunday. While Carl Thacker was up the driver cut off the engine and let the ship fall a short distance and said to Carl: "Fifty per cent of that large crowd think we are falling." Carl says, "They haven't got anything on us, 50 per cent of us think we are falling.". As every one knows, Carl's complexion is fair, but when he alighted from that air ship it was many shades lighter than ever before, however, he wasn't scared, we can prove that by him.

Two

Museum of North Texas

Call Field Museum of North Texas. The museum has gone through a number of changes since 2000 and is now part of the Museum of North Texas, at 720 Indiana Avenue in Wichita Falls. The Wichita County Archives is housed in the same building. In 2014, the World War I Jenny airplane was moved to her permanent home at the Wichita Falls Municipal Airport. (Author's collection.)

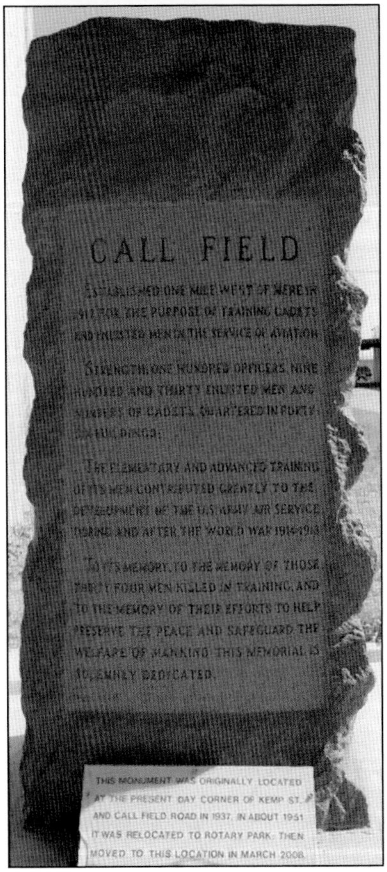

Pair of World War I Jenny Airplanes. Here, the Museum of North Texas displays a unique pair of fully operational World War I Jenny airplanes completely restored and flyable that are now housed at the Wichita Falls Municipal Airport. In addition to the Jenny, it has the Call Field staff car, also completely restored and operational. Because the planes are so rare, the choice was made to permanently ground them. Imagine observing the last flight in 2014. (Museum of North Texas.)

Call Field Marker. This monument was first located at Call Field Road in 1937 before moving to Rotary Park in 1951 and finally to the museum in 2008. It was to honor the 34 men killed in training even though records reflect some of those casualties were from the flu epidemic of 1918. (Museum of North Texas.)

Call Field Marker of Pilots Killed. A few of the names on the marker did not have accidental deaths. Those who did die in airplane crashes usually had crushed bodies and/or skulls and fatal burning. Many officers and enlisted men died of influenza in the Call Field hospital, as the epidemic spread throughout the nation. (Museum of North Texas.)

Call Field Staff Car, a 1916 Model T Ford. This model T Ford automobile has been completely restored with all original parts, even down to the quality leather seats. The US Army Air Service provided the best to training fields. (Museum of North Texas.)

Call Field Staff Car, a 1916 Model T Ford. This is another view of the Call Field staff car with the top up as this model was a convertible. The automobile is fully operational. (Museum of North Texas.)

Call Field Staff Car, Hood Ornament. This hood ornament is seen atop the radiator, which is made of brass. Hood ornaments were very elaborate on automobiles for many years. (Museum of North Texas.)

CALL FIELD STAFF CAR, STEERING COLUMN. The steering wheel is large, and the accelerator is the lever under the left side of the steering. The clutch is down below on the left, and the brake is the right pedal. The gear shift is to the right, and the siren button is on the far left. (Museum of North Texas.)

CALL FIELD STAFF CAR, DRIVER'S COMPARTMENT. Leather was standard in those days. When going for a drive, one would need to wear a scarf and goggles. (Museum of North Texas.)

Cockpit of 1917 Curtiss JN-4D Jenny. This World War I flying machine has simple controls. The Jenny was steered with a joystick and only had a few gauges. Aviation was still in its early stages, being only 14 years old when the Jenny was built. (Museum of North Texas.)

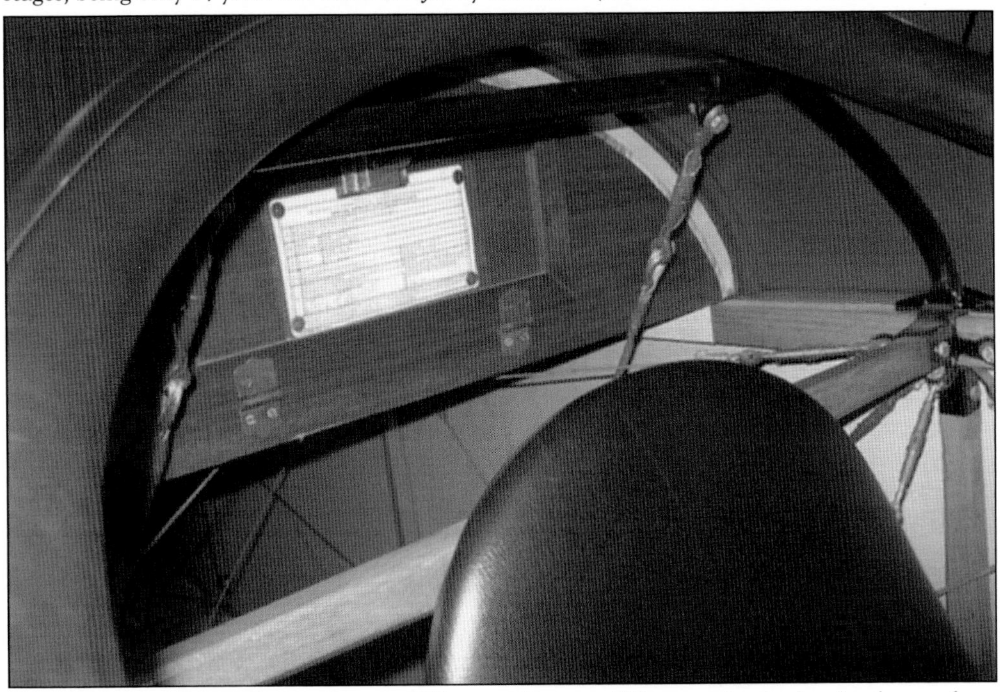

Compartment behind Pilot Seat for Homing Pigeon. When a pilot had to land away from the field, he could put a note on the pigeon and get a message back to his field so that help could be rallied. (Museum of North Texas.)

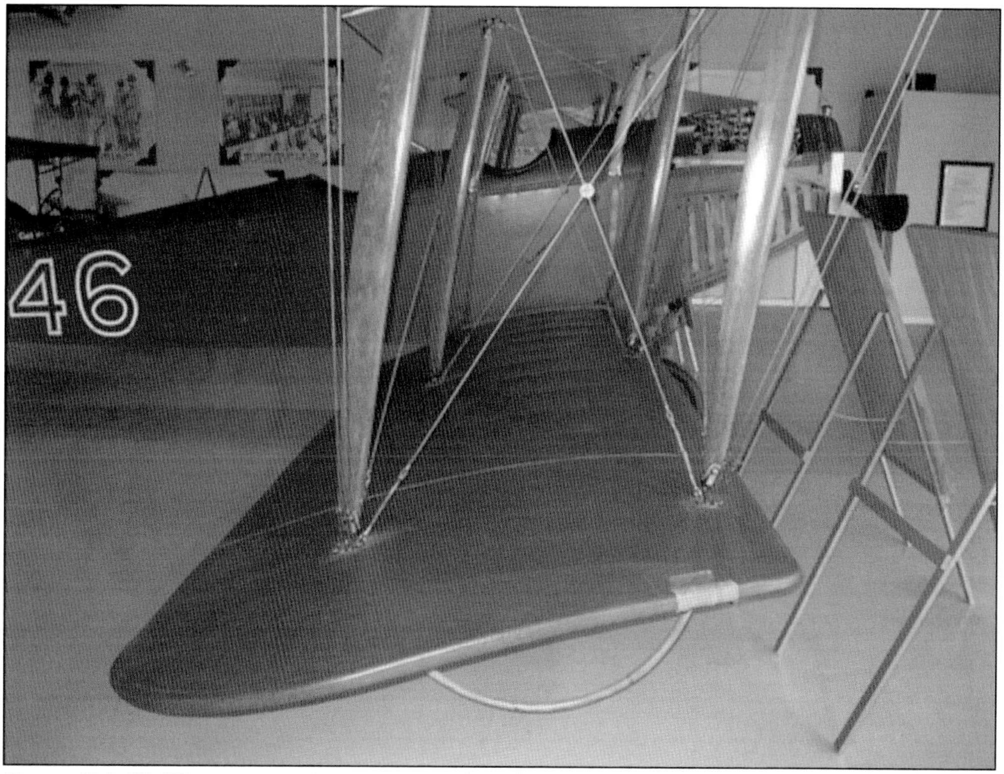

Curtis JN-4D. The wires are for structure and rigidity of the wings. The double-lift wires supported more weight pulling out of a dive due to additional Gs on the wings. The single-support wires held the wings up. The X wires between the vertical struts prevented twisting of the wings in flight. The aileron cables were inside the wings and fuselage and cannot be seen. The propeller was made of highly polished wood and had to be started by manually rotating the prop by hand. One man stood on the ground while the pilot sat in the cockpit at the controls to start the engine as it was primed. (Both, Museum of North Texas.)

Curtis JN-4D, a View of the Tail. The steel wires running down the tail wings and the ones attached to the center tail flap helped control the airplane in turns and descents. Those wires and others were operated by stick. (Museum of North Texas.)

Curtis JN-4D, Structural Control Wiring Detail. These wires are under the top wings of the airplane. Note how the wires have eyelets and hooks to make the necessary connections to help strengthen the wings. (Museum of North Texas.)

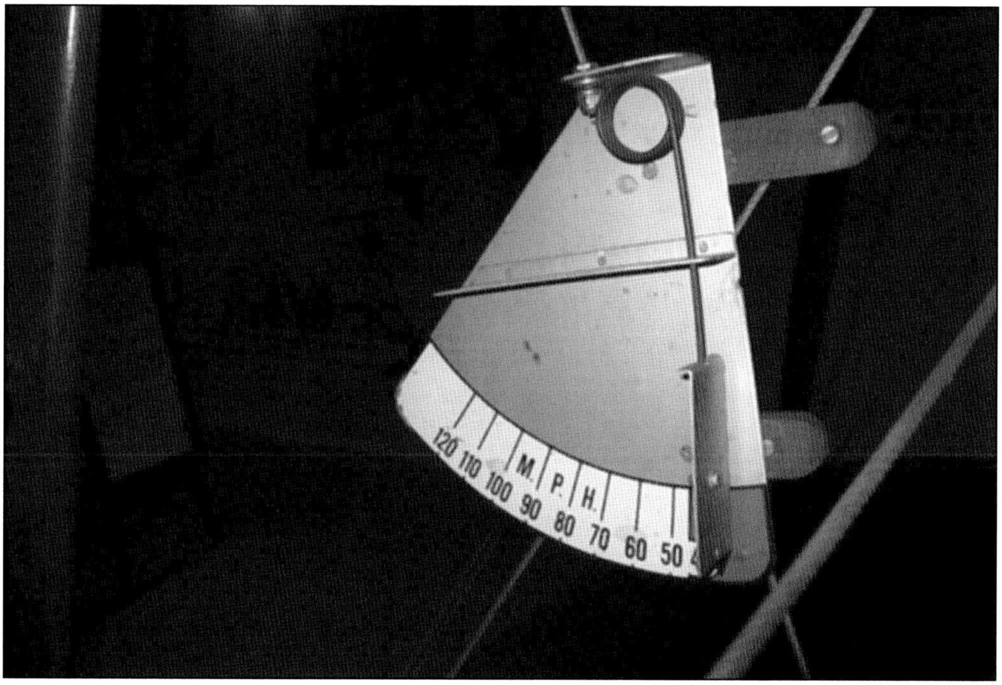

1917 Curtis JN-4D, Air-Speed Indicator. The speed indicator was mounted outside the cockpit to the left of the pilot. A top speed printed on the indicator was very optimistic for an aircraft with a solid high-end 75 miles per hour. (Museum of North Texas.)

1917 Curtis JN-4D, Fuel Gauge. The student sat in the front seat, and the instructor sat in the rear seat. In front of the first seat is the fuel gauge, which is very visible to both student and instructor. (Museum of North Texas.)

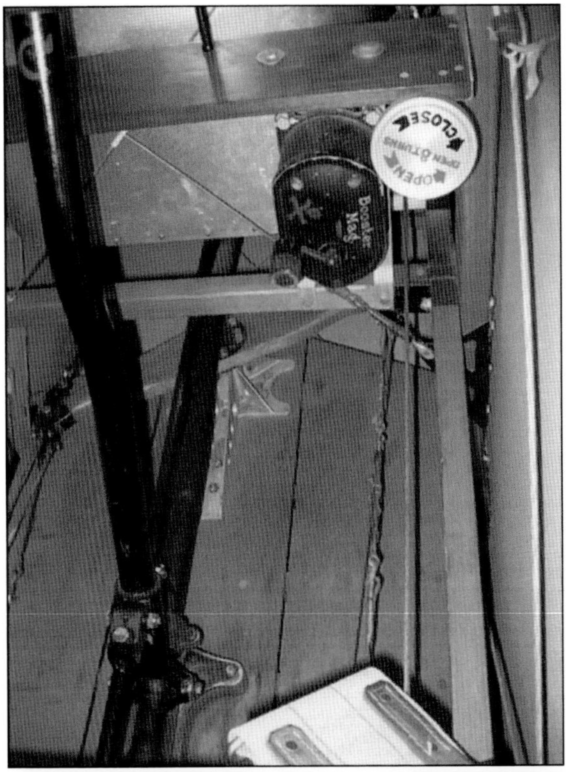

1917 CURTIS JN-4D, PEEK INTO COCKPIT. This photograph of the cockpit reveals no rudders but instead stick control. Little metal was used in these early airplanes due to weight consideration; therefore, wood was the material of choice. Add the elements of fire and wind during flight and aviators had little chance of surviving a crash. (Museum of North Texas.)

1917 JENNY, PROP DETAIL. The big nut in the center was referred to as the "Jesus nut" because if it came off during flight, it was "Oh Jesus." (Museum of North Texas.)

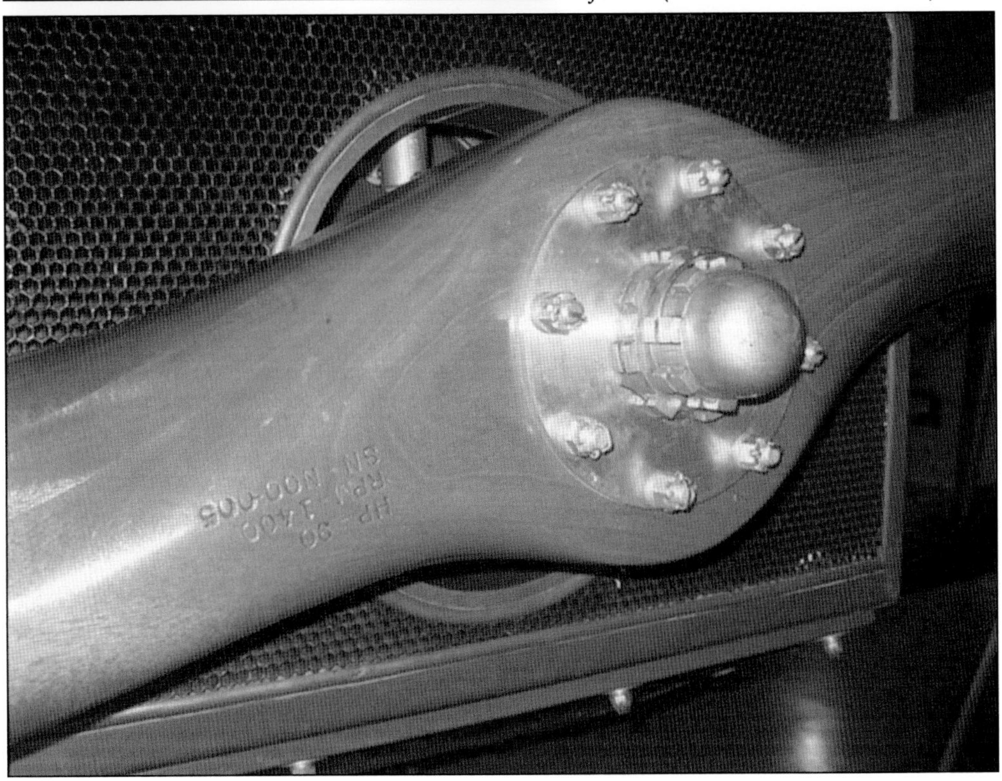

Authentic Curtis JN-4D. This image of Curtis JN-4D is not a replica but the real deal. The World War I Jenny is one of only four known to exist. It is flyable but was retired recently and moved to its permanent location at the Wichita Falls Municipal Airport. (Museum of North Texas.)

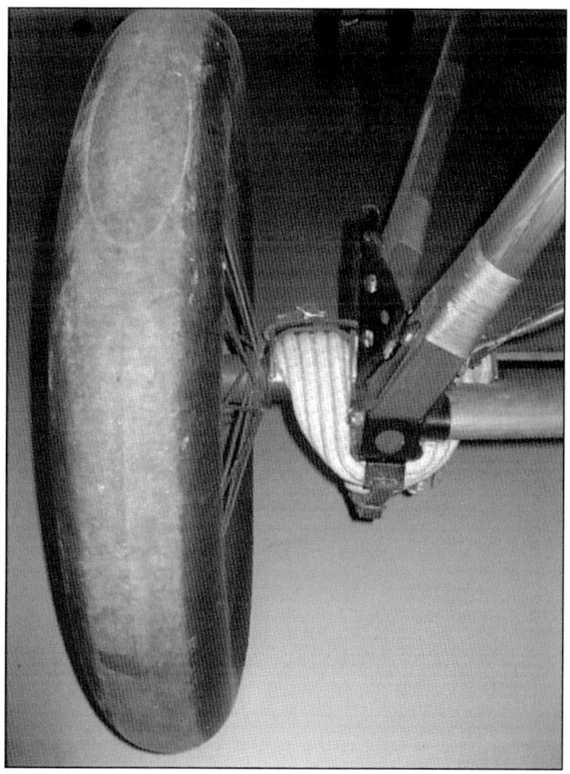

Curtis JN-4D, Front Wheel Structure. The undercarriage uses bungee cords for springing. Here, a bungee cord is a loop of many rubber bands with a woven cover that would expand and shrink as it stretched. This sort of suspension was used on most all airplanes, including the very first one. It was still in use on many light airplanes up to the 1970s. (Museum of North Texas.)

Curtiss-Wright OX-5 Engine. The power plant was a V8, liquid-cooled engine. It was rated at 90 horsepower at 1,400 revolutions per minute. It had to be serviced every five hours. For ships needing to fly longer, hand rails and running boards on either side of the engine were attached so the riding mechanic could climb up beside the engine to oil the rockers and valves in flight. (Museum of North Texas.)

Museum of North Texas. A mural was drawn on the wall behind the World War I Jenny and Model T Ford staff car. Even a desk with chairs and an old manual typewriter are displayed. (Museum of North Texas.)

Field Pack of a World War I Soldier. This pack, belonging to Pvt. Jasper Young Brown, was worn around the waist and contained shaving cream, a straight razor, comb, soap, lamp wicks, needles and a thimble, a first-aid kit, toothpaste and brush, and other assorted personal care items. Brown was wounded in France and died on April 27, 1919, in New York. (Author's collection.)

The World War I Victory Medal. Here are the front and back of the medal. It is a service medal of the US military and was designed by James Earle Fraser. The US Army published orders authorizing the medal in April 1919, and the US Navy followed in June that same year. (Museum of North Texas.)

World War I Uniforms. The Museum of North Texas has a large display of military-related items. This room has a collection of World War I uniforms and photographs on display that are related to the era. (Museum of North Texas.)

Jenny to Jet. The Museum of North Texas has come a long way from its beginnings, starting with the Call Field Museum. The Museum of North Texas obtained a T-38 Talon jet trainer and displayed it along with the World War I Jenny until it was moved to the airport. (Museum of North Texas.)

Three

Military Postcards and Posters

World War I US Army Air Service Recruiting Poster. Posters were designed for the military with the idea of attracting eligible civilian men to step forward and serve their country during the time of need. This poster makes the Army Air Service look attractive and adventurous with no hint of being in harm's way. (Carl McKinnon Collection.)

Uncle Sam. This recruiting poster was used by the military for many years, and James Montgomery Flagg drew the image of Uncle Sam in his likeness. This was the first Uncle Sam poster used by the US military. (L.L. Kaylor Collection.)

Cartoon Postcard from the US Aerial Photographers. A rare postcard depicts a photographer pointing his camera at "Fritz" while the enemy is shooting him from the rear. The card reads, "We're out to snap th' Kaiser." (Carl McKinnon Collection.)

Kitchen Patrol (KP). This postcard displays "My day on K.P." Most enlisted personnel pulled this duty often and sometimes for a week at the time. The phrase sounds special but in reality it means a lot of hard work cleaning pots, pans, and dishes, scrubbing and waxing floors, and performing other mess-hall duties from before dawn to very late at night. This was probably the very worst duty an enlisted man had to perform. This postcard covers it well. (Carl McKinnon Collection.)

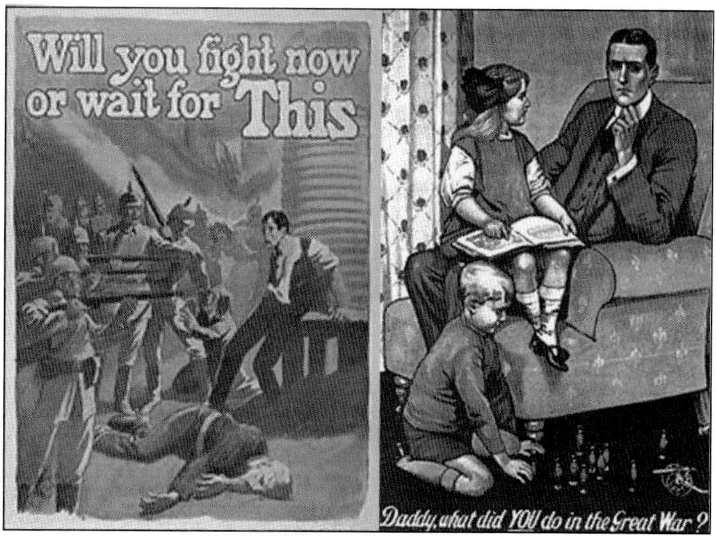

"Will You Fight Now?" This double poster challenges the patriotism of individuals as well as heads of family. The propaganda shamed many into volunteering for duty to serve their country when some were better suited to remain with family and find another way to help with the war effort. (Carl McKinnon Collection.)

POSTCARD, 1943. The wording on this postcard compares love to war by indicating the military should use the best weapons (arms) at its disposal. (Carl McKinnon Collection.)

CALL FIELD'S MAGAZINE. Call Field issued a weekly magazine in 1918. It was first titled the *Call Field Engineer* but later changed to the *Call Field Stabilizer.* The magazine not only provided local military news but also provided important news from all Army posts. Advertising was also allowed in the weekly print. (Carl McKinnon Collection.)

GI Personal Hygiene. Pictured is a postcard from World War I. Recruits came from all walks of life, and if one soldier was lazy and received a gig (demerit) for a violation, the entire company would be punished. Those who did not take baths fell down the stairs or slipped and fell in the shower, usually late at night, away from the sergeant's eyes. (Carl McKinnon Collection.)

Military Terms. This cartoon-type postcard was popular and funny to the regular soldier. It is likely that many GIs had been in at least one of these situations while courting the opposite sex. (Carl McKinnon Collection.)

DEAR JOHN. This postcard indicates that most servicemen not only obeyed the lawful orders of their superiors, but they also usually cowered to confront him on nonmilitary issues, like if a captain was trying to steal a subordinate's girlfriend. This scene is a "Dear John" letter transformed to an image with caption. (Carl McKinnon Collection.)

MUSICIANS, GOOD AND BAD. It is likely that there were many amateur musicians in the army prior to, during, and after World War I. Some were pretty good, while others were so bad that they may have fallen down stairs late at night. (Carl McKinnon Collection.)

Top Sergeant. There is probably nothing worse than getting chewed out by the first sergeant. He was called "top" mostly by Army personnel and "First Shirt" by Air Force personnel. He was an extension of the company commander and gave orders as authorized by that commander. (Carl McKinnon Collection.)

King Kong Postcard. This postcard was designed to anger a man enough to get him to enlist in the military. Of course, sex appeal always helps to get a male's attention. This image preceded the movie *King Kong* by 15 years. (Carl McKinnon Collection.)

UNIFORMS. Clothes do not make a man. Anyone who has ever served in the military has probably experienced being issued uniforms and shoes that did not fit. It became the GI's responsibility to take the ill-fitting clothing to the tailor shop for alterations. (Carl McKinnon Collection.)

PHYSICAL EXAM. Most inductees into the military felt like they were treated like cattle by the medical staff. The staff looked for those with flatfeet, heart murmurs, or other debilitating ailments. One had to be in very good health to be classified 1-A, fit for duty. (Carl McKinnon Collection.)

WORLD WAR I SOLDIER IN FIRST UNIFORM. The image depicts a left-handed salute, which indicates the recruit had a lot to learn about military discipline, customs, and procedures. (Carl McKinnon Collection.)

GETTING A LETTER. This postcard tries to express a happy feeling when receiving a letter from one's girlfriend back home. It was the reversal of a "Dear John" letter. (Carl McKinnon Collection.)

Getting a Shot. Many inductees into the military, especially during World War I and World War II, had never received any shots to ward off diseases. Being given 8 to 10 shots during one visit to the medics resulted in sore arms and buttocks. The bucket in the image is labeled "Dope," which indicated the medic inoculated them with a narcotic. (Carl McKinnon Collection.)

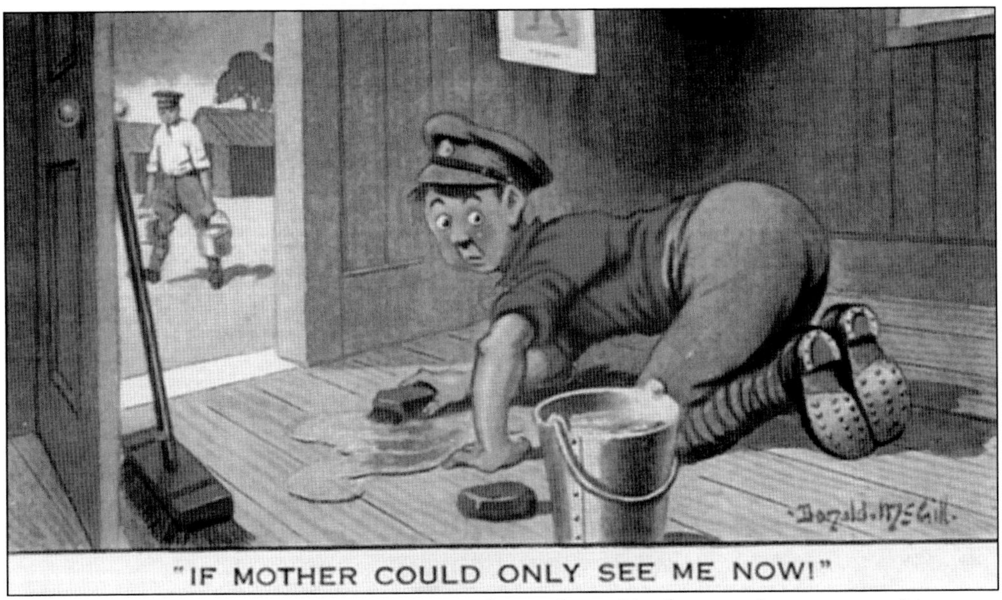

A GI Party. During training, a new recruit learned quickly that maid service was his mom, and she was not with him in the barracks. When told the first time that they were go to have a GI (Government Issue) party, it turned out to mean something totally different. Brooms, mops, buckets, soap, and brushes were issued, and most Saturdays were spent cleaning, ruining many weekends. (Carl McKinnon Collection.)

GETTING HITLER. This postcard reveals that the soldier's dream of giving Hitler a good kick is about to be interrupted by the bugler sounding reveille and rendering the alarm clock useless. (Carl McKinnon Collection.)

DOING LAUNDRY. The World War I uniforms were made of wool and shirts were flannel. This postcard indicates some soldier did not know how to wash flannel and probably knew little about washing anything to do with clothing. (Carl McKinnon Collection.)

"Which Side Are You On?" A two-sided World War I poster asks the question, "On which side of the window are you?" It indicates men should enlist for their country unless they are rooting for the Germans. (Carl McKinnon Collection.)

"We Can Do It." This is a metal poster from World War II, and many wives and daughters who did not serve in the military did their part to support the war effort by working in factories that made the war materials need to defeat the Axis powers. (Scurry County Museum.)

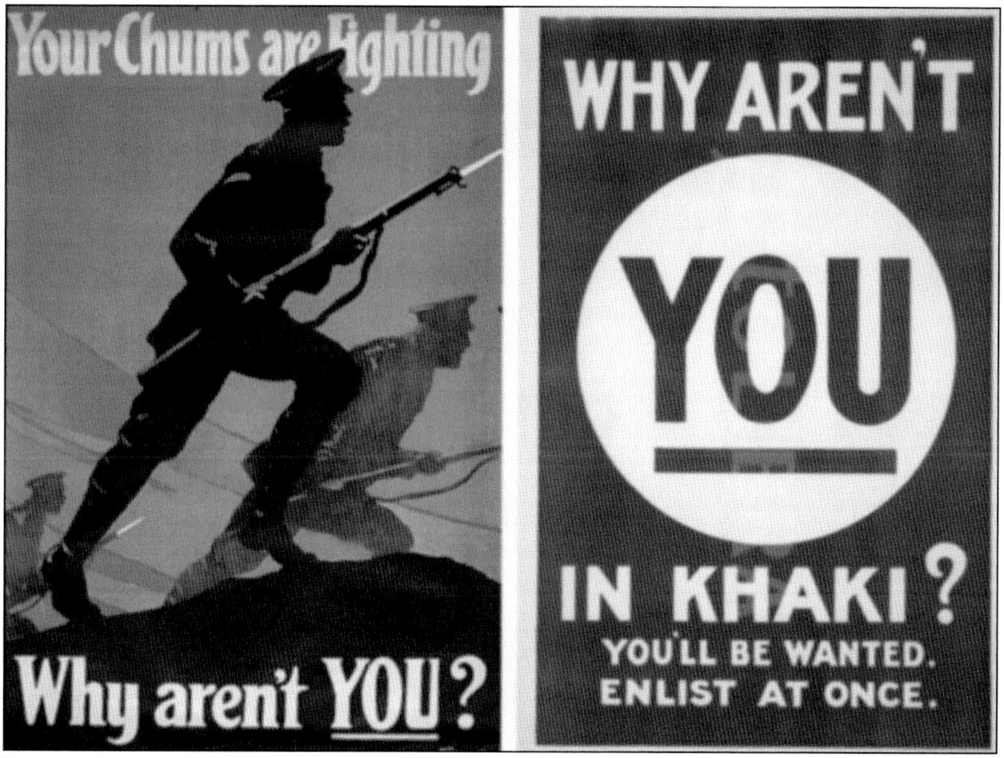

BUDDIES ENLISTED. This double-sided poster was designed to indicate that one should go along with the crowd. On one side it asks, "Your chums are fighting. Why aren't you?" On the other side, it states, "Why aren't you in khaki? You'll be wanted. Enlist Now." (Carl McKinnon Collection.)

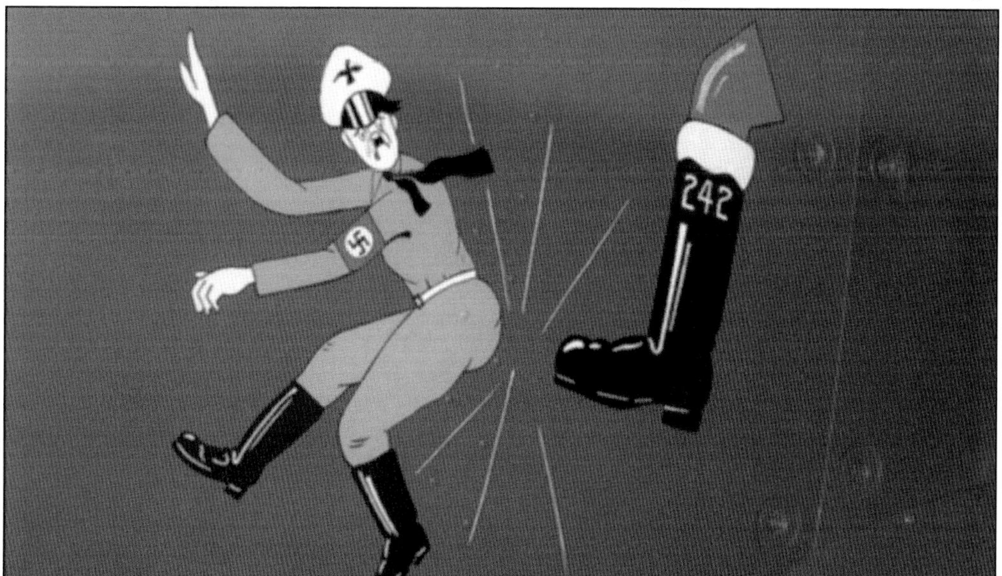

FOR HITLER. Giving Hitler a kick must have been popular during World War II as this painting was displayed under the cockpit of an airplane. The No. 242 on the boot represents the unit that the crew was assigned. (Carl McKinnon Collection.)

US Army Air Forces Recruiting Poster. There was nothing better than displaying a happy face to those who wanted to become pilots and be part of an exciting adventure in the skies. (Carl McKinnon Collection.)

Dog Tags. Here is a rare identification tag, also known as a "dog tag," that belonged to Army corporal Carl McKinnon, aerial photographer during World War I. His tag reads as follows: "Mc.Kinnon Carl L. / PVT. / 192 AERO SQDN. USA." McKinnon's grandson donated his entire collection of photographs, postcards, and documents to the Museum of North Texas. (Carl McKinnon Collection.)

Four

Birth of Sheppard Field

US Senator John Morris Sheppard. Sheppard Field, later to be redesignated as Sheppard Air Force Base, was named after the notable Texan. From left to right are Senator Sheppard, Maj. Gen. George Lynch, and Sen. A.B. Chandler. They are comparing a M1941 Johnson rifle and the M1 Garand rifle in Washington, DC, on May 29, 1940. Senator Sheppard was a direct descendant of Robert Morris, who signed the Declaration of Independence. (Author's collection.)

Farmer Takes Interest in Training Class. An instructor is explaining the schematics of a pilot's instrument panel to a group of Army aircraft technicians. It is unclear why the instructor decided to have his classroom at a nearby farm. A local farmer has decided to listen in on the session. (Museum of North Texas.)

B-17 Bomber. The Boeing B-17 Flying Fortress is a four-engine heavy bomber aircraft, primarily employed in the daylight precision strategic bombing campaign of World War II against German industrial and military targets. The B-17 also participated in the war in the Pacific early in World War II. (Museum of North Texas.)

B-24 Crew Training Sheppard Field. The Consolidated Aircraft Corporation's B-24 showed improved range and payload capabilities over the B-17. The performance was, in most respects, quite comparable, and one might question why the B-24 was built at all since the B-24 was more difficult to fly and cost more than the B-17. (Courtesy Museum of North Texas.)

Air-Traffic Control Training. A high-ranking officer is seated while being briefed by air-traffic control personnel while a soldier in the pit uses a wooden rod to move a model airplane down the taxiway. It could be the replay of an accident. (Museum of North Texas.)

SHEPPARD FIELD'S FIRST BUILDING. The public affairs office at Sheppard Field apparently took pride in running right out to take a photograph of its first structure, an outhouse, dated May 1941. Creature comforts are important to the Army. It does appear to have been well built with good air ventilation and looks to be a two-seat facility. (Museum of North Texas.)

OFFICERS GRADUATING FROM AIRPLANE MECHANICS SCHOOL. Pictured are, from left to right, (first row) Warrant Officer James W. Walker, Capt. William R. Chenoweth, Lt. A.R. J. Friedman, and Lt. Wray E. Dudley; (second row) Lt. Herschel W. Conner, Warrant Officer Clark C. Mathison, Warrant Officer Arthur E. Kline, Warrant Officer Galen E. Turner, and Capt. Lomax Gwathmey. They would be transferring next to flight engineering school in 1943. (Museum of North Texas.)

BEECHCRAFT AT-11. The pilot heads his bombing training mission out over the vast West Texas prairies to find its target as the bombardier student and instructor ready the bombsight in the nose of the plane for the early-morning mission. (US Air Force.)

THE B-10 MARTIN. The B-10 began a revolution in bomber design. Its all-metal monoplane build, along with its closed cockpits, rotating gun turrets, retractable landing gear, internal bomb bay, and full-engine cowlings, would become the standard for bomber design worldwide for decades and made all existing bombers obsolete. It had a crew of four: pilot, copilot, nose gunner, and fuselage gunner. (Authors collection.)

Boeing B-29 Superfortress. Most B-29s carried eight .50-caliber machine guns in remote-controlled turrets, two .50- caliber machine guns, one 20-millimeter cannon in a tail turret, and up to 20,000 pounds of bombs. Instructors at Sheppard Field trained mechanics on the B-29. It was the Bockscar B-29 that dropped the "Fat Man" atomic bomb on Nagasaki, Japan, on August 9, 1945. (US Air Force.)

French Language Class at Sheppard Field. A selected number of army personnel attended French Language School at Sheppard Field in preparation for deployment to France during World War II. (Museum of North Texas.)

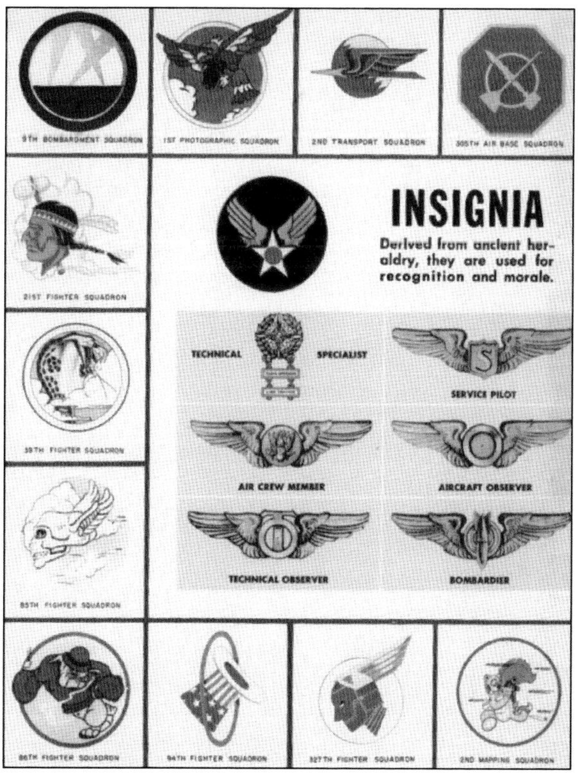

Insignia of World War II. This poster displays the various insignia rewarded for recognition and morale of the troops. Every flyer had a special wings insignia from pilot to bombardier. (Author's collection.)

Marching in the Barracks Area Sheppard Field. This 1943 postcard was stamped and mailed by the post office to an undisclosed address. The image shows many companies of troops marching through the barracks area. Many of those barracks were still standing in the mid-1980s. (Author's collection.)

Norden Bombsight. Here is a tachymetric bombsight used by the Army Air Forces and Navy during World War II, the Korean War, and Vietnam to help the crew of aircraft in dropping bombs accurately. The bombsight was an analog computer that constantly calculated the bomb's trajectory based on current flight conditions, and it had a linkage to the bomber's autopilot that let it react quickly and accurately to changes in the wind or other effects. (Museum of North Texas.)

P-38 LIGHTENING. The Lockheed P-38 Lightning was a World War II American fighter aircraft that had distinctive twin booms and a single, central nacelle containing the cockpit and armament. It was named "fork-tailed devil" by the Luftwaffe and "two planes, one pilot" by the Japanese. The aircraft had a number of roles, including dive bombing, level bombing, ground attack, night fighting, and photograph reconnaissance missions and had extensive work as a long-range escort fighter when equipped with drop tanks under its wings. (Author's collection.)

P-38 LIGHTENING'S COCKPIT. The instrument panel inside the cockpit of the P-38 was uncomplicated for the pilot once he was trained in the various functions of the aircraft. This fast-flying airplane was one of the best experiences for an Army Air Corps pilot during World War II. (Air Force Museum.)

The Curtiss P-40 Warhawk. The Curtiss P-40 Warhawk was an American single-engine, single-seat, all-metal fighter and ground-attack aircraft. The Warhawk was used by most Allied powers during World War II and remained in frontline service until the end of the war. (Air Force Museum.)

PBY Seaplanes. Two hundred PBY seaplanes are shown moored on Lake Worth in November 1940 at Fort Worth, Texas. Sheppard Field trained technicians to repair them as they were in the Air Corps inventory. Consolidated Aircraft transferred these planes from San Diego to the East Coast, and Fort Worth was a good place to layover. This transfer was kept secret as the PBYs were being flown to Great Britain. (Museum of North Texas.)

Plastic Department. Sheppard Field had a plastic assembly department during World War II. This scene shows what appears to be fuel filters and plastic bottles for undisclosed usage. Pictured are two corporals sitting at the assembly table and a sergeant. (Museum of North Texas.)

Sheppard Field World War II. The inspection branch instructors and students are performing a 50-hour inspection on a B-25 Bomber. There appears to be six soldiers working on this inspection. (Museum of North Texas.)

SHEPPARD FIELD ELECTRIC BRANCH. This World War II training facility was responsible for teaching students to work on electrical motors. They are working on 24-volt Starter Motors. The chalkboard lists instructors as Staff Sergeant Ritthaler, Sergeant Fink, and Sergeant Murphy. (Museum of North Texas.)

VIEW FROM ABOVE. An aerial view of the parking ramp at Sheppard Air Force Base reveals a variety of World War II–era planes, including the B-17 bomber. Visitors have arrived by bus and personal vehicle to attend the air show. (Museum of North Texas.)

T-6 TEXAN. The North American T-6 Texan, manufactured by Beechcraft, was a single-engine advanced trainer aircraft used to train fighter pilots of the US Army Air Forces. Mechanics were trained at Sheppard Field. (Air Force Museum.)

TRAINING DISPLAY BOARD, SHEPPARD FIELD. The instructor is pointing to a hydraulic and oxygen setup. The black box is an A-14 regulator, which reduces the 600-pounds-per-square-inch pressure from the tanks to the appropriate amount needed for breathing based on altitude. Before that, pilots used masks with the bladder hanging below them, and the pilot had to manually adjust the oxygen flow. (Museum of North Texas.)

Wood Shop at Sheppard Field. These soldiers are using a wood press to secure a wooden propeller, while another appears to be shaving it with a wood chisel. They may be making a new prop or repairing a damaged one. (Museum of North Texas.)

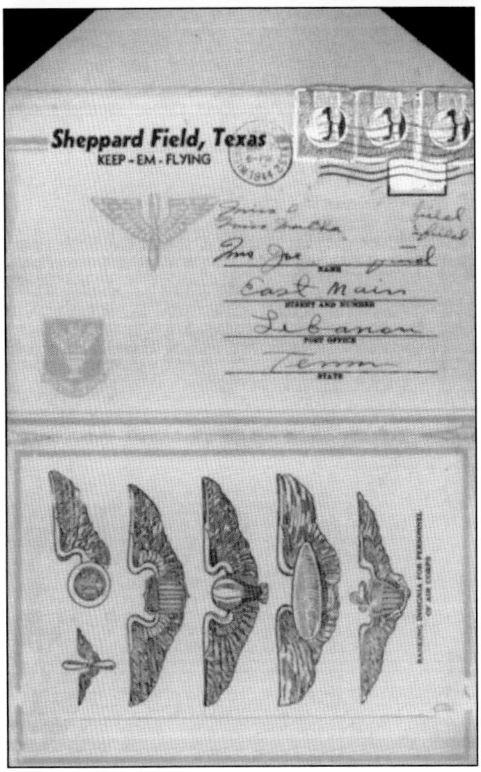

Sheppard Field Mailer. This pamphlet had postcards inside and was mailed from Sheppard Field by Pvt. Walter Smithwick Jr. to his father's sister and two cousins in Lebanon, Tennessee, in May 1944. Recently, the pamphlet, with postcards intact, was located in Madison, Alabama, as a rare book. Walter Smithwick survived the war and died in 1997. (Author's collection.)

Five

Female Pilots of World War II

Capt. Edith McKanna. Edith McKanna is seen standing beside her Eaglerock airplane and her Lincoln automobile at the airport in Wichita Falls, Texas. She became the first Texas female licensed pilot in 1929, first to own her own plane, and the first female charter member of the Ninety-Nine Club (first 99 female pilots in America). During World War II, she was a captain in the Civil Air Patrol (CAP) and served as liaison with the Army Air Corps. She donated her plane to the war effort. (Scurry County Museum.)

Edith McKanna and Husband. Edith and her husband, James McKanna, are standing beside her Eaglerock airplane. They were oil operators based out of Wichita Falls. James died of heart failure in 1932, and Edith carried on the business, flying her airplane to help run it as well. (Scurry County Museum.)

Captain McKanna by Her Airplane. She had imprinted on the side of her Eaglerock plane, "Mrs. Jas E. McKanna, Wichita Falls, Texas." She logged well over 3,000 hours of flight time in various airplanes. (Scurry County Museum.)

McKanna in Buggy. Edith and two girlfriends had their photograph taken in this prop buggy with a drop cloth of a wooded scene, quite a contrast from the treeless prairie of her ranch in West Texas. (Scurry County Museum.)

Wichita Falls. Edith and James McKanna lived in Wichita Falls, which was the heart of the early oil boom. The couple bought leases on lands where oil was likely to be produced. (Scurry County Museum.)

Civil Air Patrol Captain McKanna. Here, Capt. Edith McKanna is shown sitting on the tail wing of an airplane during World War II. She donated her plane to the war effort. For three years, she served with the rank of captain at the Air Force headquarters as a liaison for the CAP and the Army Air Corps. (Scurry County Museum.)

In Uniform. Captain McKanna in a khaki uniform is standing by a coup automobile displaying the CAP emblem. The photograph was taken at Sheppard Field, Texas. (Scurry County Museum.)

OFFICERS' CLUB AT SHEPPARD FIELD. Captain McKanna and friends are photographed at happy hour in the Officers' Club at Sheppard Field following a meeting with the Army Air Corps commander. Captain McKanna is seated on the left. (Scurry County Museum.)

CAPTAIN MCKANNA ENTERING HER AIRPLANE. This image was used by the Army Air Corps to show the official uniform for women, which was the same for men except that skirts or culottes were substituted for trousers. Slacks were optional for women's service uniform when flying or partaking in field activity. The uniform includes a blouse and brown military shoes with buckles. (Scurry County Museum.)

B-17 Pilots Posing. These pilots are standing in front of a B-17. From left to right are Blanche Osborn, Betty Clements, Mary Parker Gair, Virginia Archer, Doris Bristol, Peg Kirchner, Roberta Mundt, Pat Bowser, Virginia Broome, Ann Waldner, Frances Green, Helen Dettweiler, Lucille Friesen, Dawn Rochow, Charlotte Mitchell, and Eugenie Garvin. (Avenger Field Museum.)

Vultee BT-13B Valiant Basic Trainer. The Valiant was the basic trainer used by the Women Airforce Service Pilots (WASP) during training. It represented the second of the three stages of pilot training: primary, basic, and advanced. Compared with the primary trainers in use at the time, it was considerably more complex. (US Air Force.)

Pilot Elizabeth L. Gardner. Elizabeth L. Gardner, WASP, is seen at the controls of a B-26 Marauder. Pilot Gardner takes a look around before sending her plane streaking down the runway in 1944 as part of the WASP project of having women pilots move aircraft on the home front to free up more male pilots for combat duty. (US Air Force.)

Stearman PT-13. The PT-13 was typical of the biplane primary trainer used during World War II and was a trainer used by the WASP. The Boeing Airplane Company purchased the Stearman Company in 1938. (US Air Force.)

STEARMAN PT-13's COCKPIT. The airplane was flown by stick and rudder pedals. The instrument panel showed the climb rate, an altimeter, a clock, and other obvious controls. (US Air Force.)

WASP FLORENCE MILLER WATSON. WASP Florence Miller Watson is shown here preparing a P-51D-5NA for a ferry flight from the factory in 1944. She was one of 28 women qualified for the original Women's Auxiliary Ferrying Squadron. In 1944, she was a test pilot in a secretive program to develop radar. She was qualified to fly the P-39, P-40, P-47, and P-51. (US Air Force.)

Tow Target Pilots. Many WASPs flew A-25s and B-26s on tow-target missions to train aerial gunners. Here, these pilots are given a mission briefing by a captain. (US Air Force.)

WASP Helen W. Snapp. This is the Curtiss A-25 tow target plane flown by WASP Helen W. Snapp. Women Airforce Service Pilots used A-25s to fly gunnery training missions. The flights involved towing a target sleeve on a long wire past ground anti-aircraft gunners, who then shot at the sleeve with live ammunition. (US Air Force.)

Nancy Harkness Love. Nancy was one of two female pilots to be the first to fly the Boeing B-17 Flying Fortress. She and Betty Gillies, her copilot, were scheduled to fly the *Queen Bee* to England but the flight was canceled. (US Air Force.)

Early Pilots of B-17 Flying Fortress. Betty Gillies was one of the first, along with Nancy Love, to fly the B-17 Flying Fortress. (US Air Force.)

WASP Flying the B-17 Flying Fortress. These four female pilots have completed ferry training in a B-17. From left to right, Frances Green, Margaret "Peg" Kirchner, Ann Waldner, and Blanche Osborn are leaving their plane, *Pistol Packin' Mama.* (US Air Force.)

WASP Ferry Pilots. These six Women Airforce Service Pilots are seen wearing the different uniforms female pilots adorned when flying or on the ground. (US Air Force.)

Final Group Photograph. Here, women join for one last group photograph as WASP was disbanded on December 20, 1944, which brought an end to the brave sacrifices made by women who flew every type of aircraft in the Army Air Corps inventory. (US Air Force.)

The Congressional Gold Medal. On March 11, 2010, the first female military pilots received the Congressional Gold Medal at a ceremony in the Capitol. When the WASP was disbanded, there was little fanfare. This ceremony was a way to make things right for the trailblazers, said Air Force secretary Michael B. Donley. Thirty-eight WASP were killed during the war due to accidents: 11 in training and 27 as active pilots. (US Air Force.)

JEAN LYON. She learned to fly and received her commercial pilot's license at a young age in Oklahoma City and became a charter member of the Ninety-Nine Club. Its headquarters and museum are located at Will Rogers Airport in Oklahoma City. Pioneer pilot Jim Forman was trained by Jean and received his commercial license at age 16. (Jim Foreman collection.)

SABRINA JACKINTELL. Sabrina Jackintell was another pioneer female aviator. Her real fame came as a high-altitude record-setting glider pilot. On Valentine's Day 1979, Sabrina established a women's world altitude record, reaching 41,460 feet. Her absolute altitude record has never been broken. (Jim Foreman collection.)

INSPECTIONS. Ferry pilots are standing for inspection by Cmdr. Jackie Cochran in 1943. These WASP trainees are learning to fly B-17 bombers. (US Air Force.)

JACKIE COCHRAN. Here is Chuck Yeager with Jackie Cochran at the controls of a Canadair F-86 Sabre jet. With the tutoring from pilots like Yeager, Jackie soon became an accomplished jet pilot. (US Air Force.)

CAPT. EDITH MCKANNA ON BAGGAGE CART AT TRAIN DEPOT. At the end of World War II, Edith returned to her family ranch near Fluvanna in Scurry County, Texas. She no longer had her husband but continued in the oil business. (Scurry County Museum.)

CAPT. EDITH MCKANNA ON BUSINESS TRIP. Edith did not wear a flight suit when she flew to various locations to secure oil leases. She dressed like a lady by wearing fashionable attire, heels, and white gloves every time she went to the oil fields. (Scurry County Museum.)

Oil Wells. Here, Edith McKanna is shown checking one of her oil wells in her white gloves, which became a trademark. Always the lady, she was well respected by oil-rig employees when she arrived. She was a trendsetter for women in the Army as well as civilian women in the 1950s. (Scurry County Museum.)

Gasoline Delivery Truck for Magnolia Petroleum Company. Edith McKanna was a large stockholder in Magnolia. Following her service during World War II, she returned to West Texas and organized the Imperial Oil Company for Eastern interests and took an active role in management, securing oil leases and drilling operations. She maintained her flying skills, traveling to the oil strikes while the "deal was hot." (Scurry County Museum.)

Six

Sheppard Becomes an Air Force

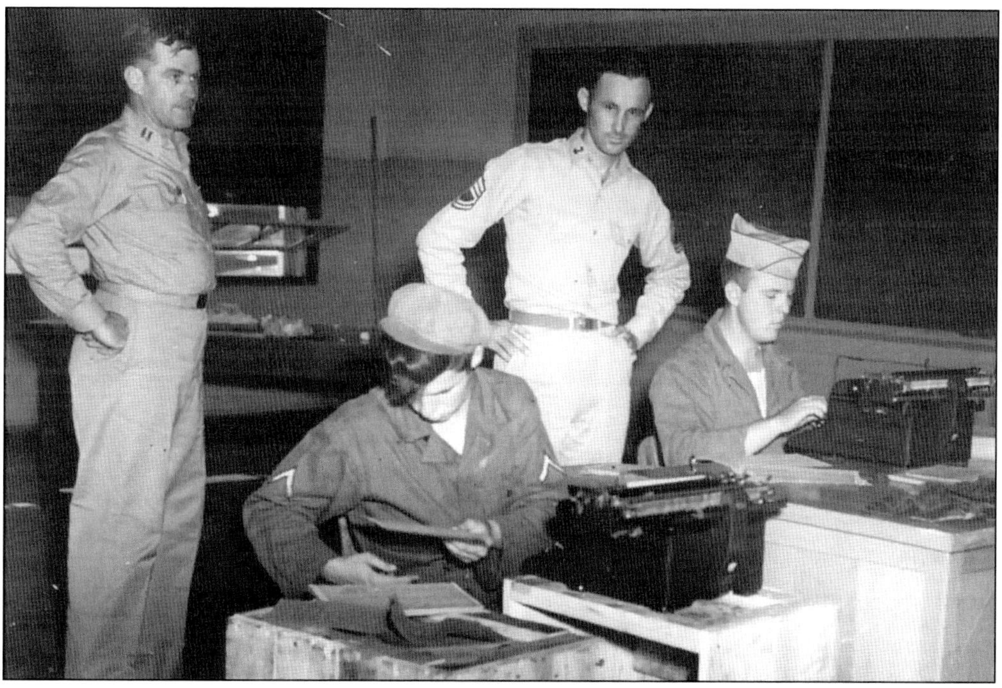

August 19, 1948. Pictured is the Orderly Room's office furniture on the first day of business on August 19, 1948, at Sheppard Air Force Base, Texas. When the US Air Force was split from the US Army on July 26, 1947, it kept the US Army's enlisted ranks. On April 24, 1952, Air Force Regulation 39-36 changed the name of the enlisted US Air Force rank to airman for E-1 through E-4, sergeant E-5, technical sergeant E-6, master sergeant E-7, senior master sergeant E-8, and chief master sergeant E-9. (Museum of North Texas.)

AN AIR FORCE RECRUITING FLOAT AT A PARADE, 1948. This Air Force recruiting float from the 3750th Training Wing, Sheppard Air Force Base, participates in the Armistice Day Parade on November 11, 1948, in Wichita Falls, Texas. Today, Armistice Day is known as Veterans Day. (Museum of North Texas.)

TRAINING MISSION. A training mission is pictured at Sheppard Air Force base on July 27, 1949. These soldiers are being taught the best defensive action after being spotted by enemy aircraft by hitting the ground to make smaller targets when being strafed or bombed. (Museum of North Texas.)

FRONT GATE ENTRANCE OF SHEPPARD AIR FORCE BASE. The Sheppard Air Force Base entrance sign at the front gate is shown here. Shortly after opening, the base became the world's largest military training system—the entrance sign advertised that as factual. (Museum of North Texas.)

HOMECOMING PARADE. Sheppard Air Force Base personnel participate in the Midwestern University Homecoming Parade in downtown Wichita Falls on a rainy October 27, 1951. Good rapport between the base and community was not only important but also routinely accomplished. (Museum of North Texas.)

Insignia. The staff sergeants are wearing army-type rank insignia, dating the photograph between 1948 and 1952; they are administrative personnel from the civil affairs branch. The captain has Army Air Corps wings but no aviator wings. The model planes on the desk are of World War II vintage. From left to right are the P-51, PBY Navy and Army Air Corps, B-24, B-17, PQ-14 (used for gunnery practice), and an A-26 low-level attack bomber. The model planes were props for a newspaper photo opportunity. (Museum of North Texas.)

Inspecting a Squadron. A commander is inspecting a squadron of Air Force personnel on July 21, 1952. The enlisted men are no longer wearing the Army rank insignia but the Air Force enlisted rank insignia that was approved on April 24, 1952. (Museum of North Texas.)

Briefing Local Scouts. This unidentified staff sergeant is briefing these local Scouts on the different types of aircraft utilized at Sheppard Air Force Base from a map-type display of the various aircraft on the tarmac. (Museum of North Texas.)

Sheppard Air Force Base Field Repair Tent. This crew has just towed an aircraft and backed it into a tent for maintenance. The hot temperatures and dusty, dry weather made it almost impossible during summer months to do repairs in the open. (Museum of North Texas.)

"Welcome to Sheppard A.F.B." Flight-line service technicians are standing on a boarding ramp with "Welcome to Sheppard A.F.B." imprinted on the side; the photograph is dated March 13, 1952. Did these men jump the gun on wearing the new US Air Force enlisted rank of airman? The Air Force regulation requiring the change was not approved until April 24, 1952. It is likely that an order was given by someone in authority to make the change in advance. (Museum of North Texas.)

Sheppard Air Force Base Baseball Team. This Sheppard Air Force Base baseball team has won a championship in 1952. Standing are, from left to right, Captains Ross and Wilde, Sergeants Perry and Richardson, Private First Class Eubela, Corporal Baumann, Staff Sergeant McGill, and Technical Sergeant Roth. Only two can be identified kneeling, Sergeant Pevey (far left) and Private First Class Jones (far right). The photograph was taken during the transition period as private first class and corporal are Army ranks. (Museum of North Texas.)

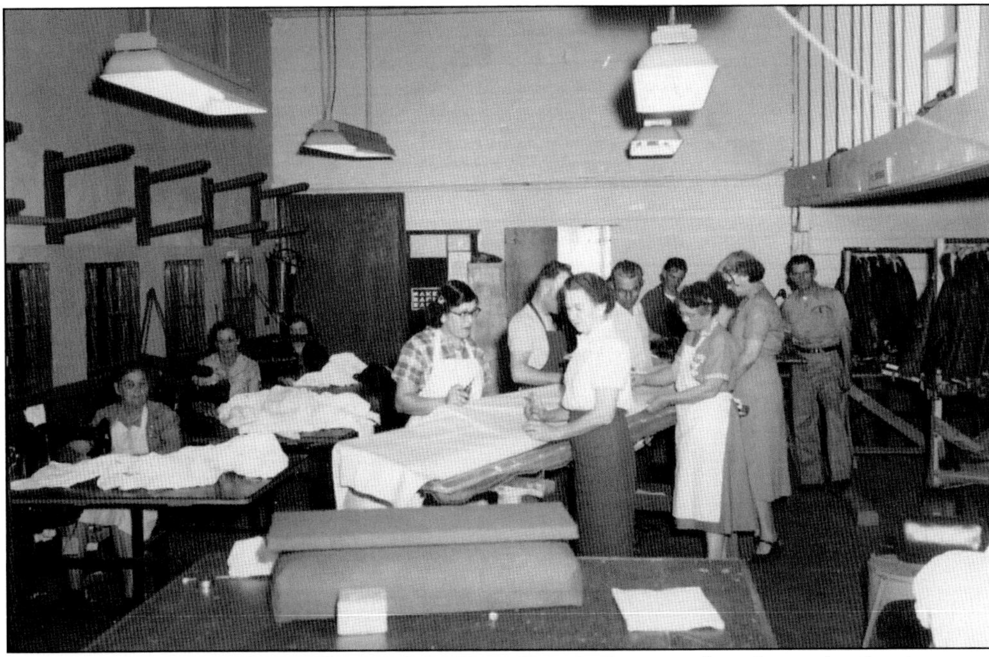

LAUNDRY AND TAILOR SHOP. Sheppard Air Force Base had its own laundry and tailor shop, and it was especially busy removing old Army stripes for the new airmen stripes when this image was taken on April 3, 1952. Employees are working at a cutting table while seamstresses are busy at their sewing machines. (Museum of North Texas.)

LAUNDRY DAY. This sergeant of the 3750th Training Wing is dropping a bundle of clothing into the laundry chute on July 17, 1953. One was required to put a slip with his identity inside the bundle. The laundry had a drop chute and a cashier window to pick up the fresh laundry and pay the bill. (Museum of North Texas.)

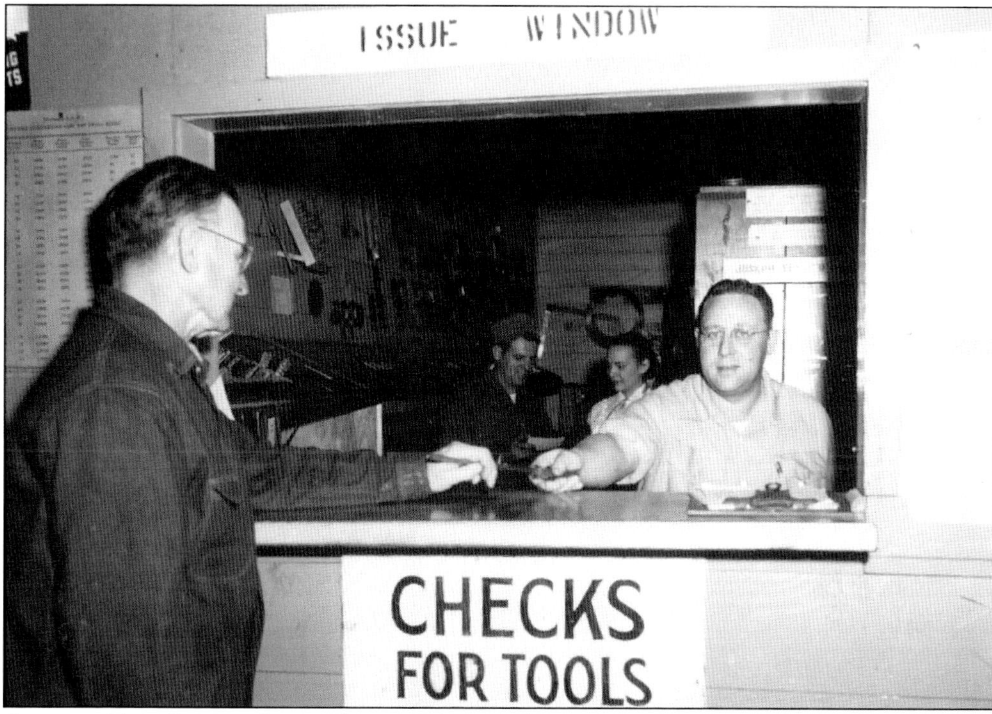

Central Tool Room. This mechanic of the 3750th Training Wing is checking out a screwdriver from the tool room on April 3, 1952, from a civil service employee. A central tool room was utilized throughout the military to prevent lost or misplaced tools. (Museum of North Texas.)

First National Bank at Sheppard Air Force Base. First National Bank of Wichita Falls opened a branch bank at Sheppard Air Force Base in the early 1950s to better serve the local military establishment. The bank leased this small structure on base property. Note its hours of operation. (Museum of North Texas.)

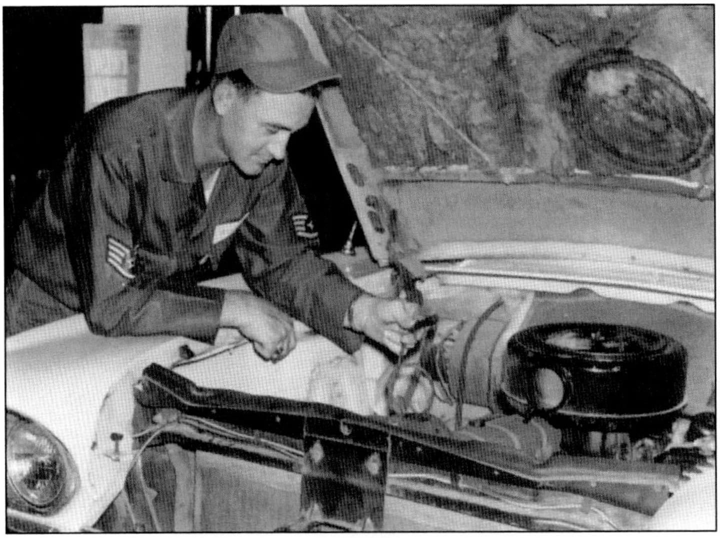

Auto Enthusiasts. The base, like all military bases, had an auto hobby shop to serve the needs of those with privately owned vehicles. One could use the shop free of charge to do tune-ups, oil changes, and overall engine care, but individuals were responsible for their own parts. This sergeant is doing a tune-up on his vehicle. (Museum of North Texas.)

Convair B-36 Peacemaker. These instructors and students are working on the Convair B-36 Peacemaker. The aircraft was built with a fuselage designed to haul nuclear weapons (hydrogen bombs) and operated by the US Air Force from 1949 to 1959. The B-36 had the largest aircraft piston engines ever made. There is not a single flyable B-36 left in the world. The aircraft was replaced by the jet-powered Boeing B-52 Stratofortress. (Museum of North Texas.)

Women in the Air Force (WAF). The ladies shown here are members of the WAF. They are all airmen 3rd class (later renamed airwomen) and have recently arrived at Sheppard to attend training in the medical field. Their uniforms, even purses, are US Air Force issued. They are lined up to draw necessary gear needed for training. (Museum of North Texas.)

Paving the Streets. The streets in the barracks area of 3750th Technical Training Wing are being repaved by civil service construction workers of the Civil Engineers Squadron on April 21, 1954. Many of these barracks were still standing, with some being utilized, in the 1980s. (Museum of North Texas.)

Directing Aircraft Traffic. The control tower stands prominently near the flight line in the late 1950s. Helicopters, hangars, warehouses, and other base facilities can be viewed in this photograph. Elevators were not en vogue in those days, so stairs had to be utilized to get to the tower. (Museum of North Texas.)

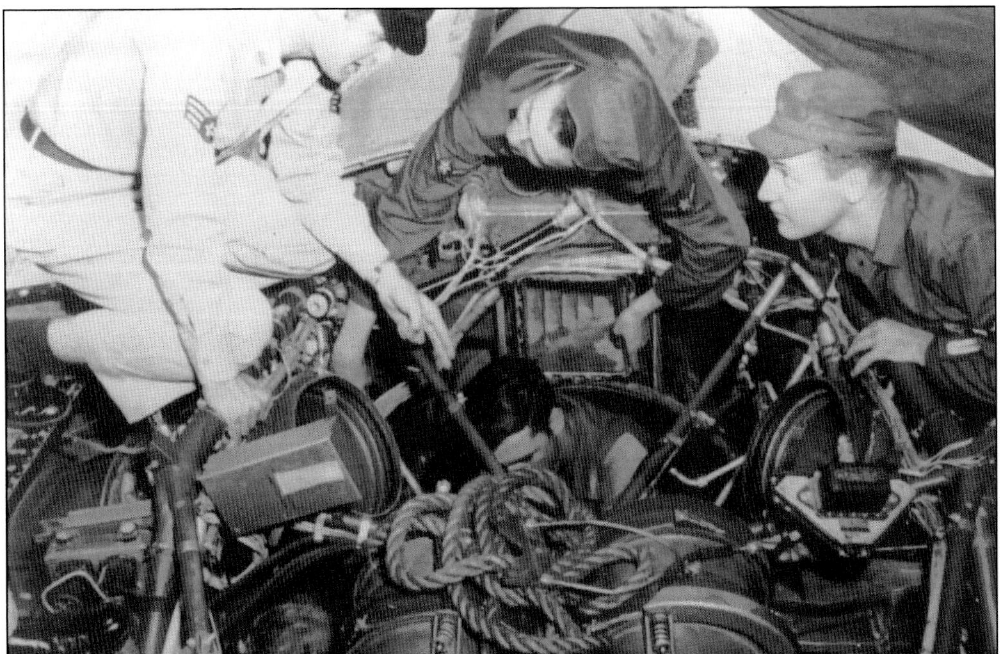

How to Replace an Engine. This instructor is pointing out to airmen students the correct way to remove or replace a very large and heavy engine from underneath the hood of a big vehicle. One airman is working underneath while the others are topside. (Museum of North Texas.)

C.R. Kennedy. Kennedy, a female instructor, is explaining to students that the main switch must be turned off before disconnecting any components of this aircraft's hydraulic system. (Museum of North Texas.)

How to Use a Crane. These students are learning how to use a crane to lower a jeep onto a pallet so it can be tied down and lifted again for aerial transport. (Museum of North Texas.)

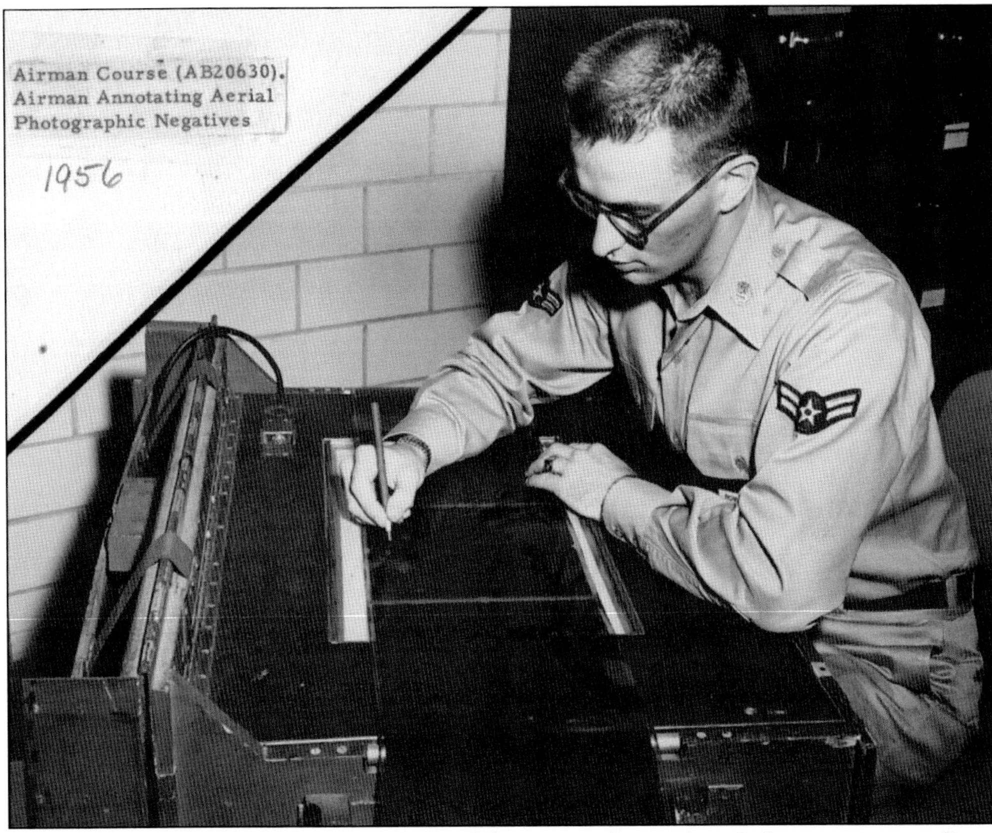

How to Annotate Aerial Photographic Negatives. An unidentified airman is attending a course to learn how to annotate aerial photographic negatives. These were the airmen who wrote the captions at the top or bottom of these military images. (Museum of North Texas.)

Inspection Team, 1956. An inspection team came to Sheppard Air Force Base in 1956 to check the readiness of flight training of the 3750th Flight Training Wing. The wing received a proficiency rating after all aspects of flight training, including equipment and personnel, were observed and noted. (Museum of North Texas.)

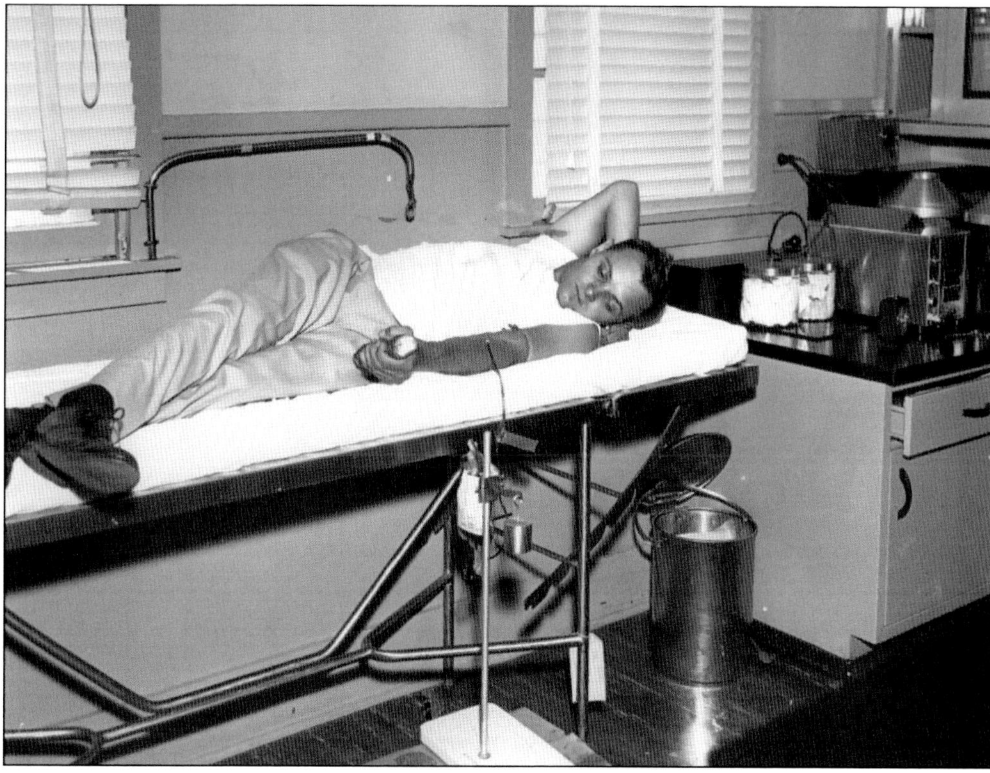

BLOOD DRIVE, 1956. An airman is donating blood during a blood drive in 1956 at the Sheppard Air Force Base Hospital. Due to the hazards of military life, blood is always in demand. (Museum of North Texas.)

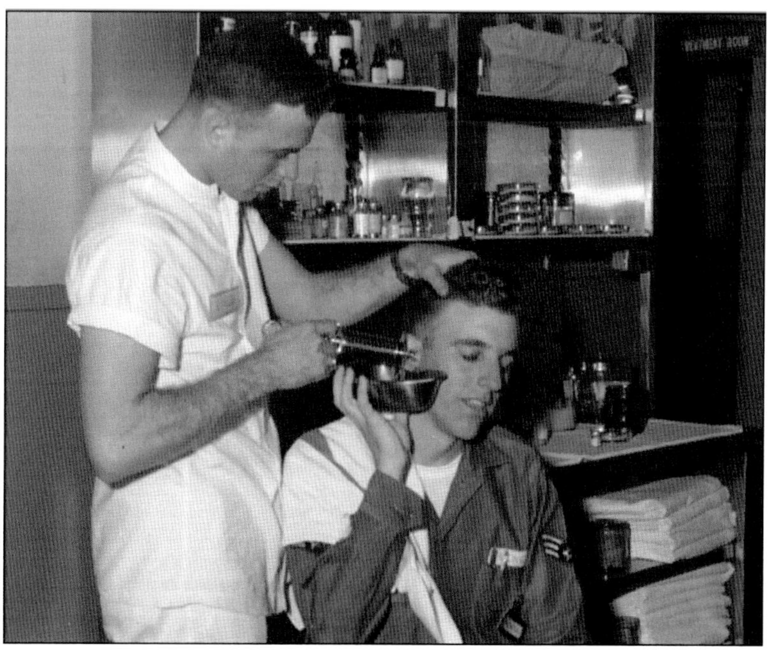

HELP FROM A MEDICAL TECHNICIAN. This medical technician is using an instrument to flush an airman's ears with warm water as the patient holds a small tub to catch the liquid. It was a procedure to flush earwax from the eardrum. (Museum of North Texas.)

Saudi Arabian Prince Visits Sheppard Air Force Base. These officers from Saudi Arabia were part of the early flight-training programs at Sheppard Air Force Base. Upon graduation, the students received US Air Force wings as well as wings from their own country. The officer is explaining producers to a prince from an Air Force manual. (Museum of North Texas.)

Foreign Officers from Saudi Arabia. These foreign officers seem to be intrigued by the same manual as previously shown to the prince. It is unclear as to the nature of the discussion. The men were a few from the many North Atlantic Treaty Organization (NATO) countries that relied on the US Air Force to provide the best training in the world. (Museum of North Texas.)

Reserve Officers Training Corps. In 1955, Sheppard Air Force Base became host, in addition to its routine mission of training, to 22 college and university Reserve Officers Training Corps (ROTC) for summer encampment that began on June 19. This was a four-week training schedule for more than 100 students. Here, Flight A is marching to class on a clear summer morning. (Museum of North Texas.)

The Mechanics of a Jet Engine. Sergeant Lyle, the instructor, is pointing out the mechanics of a jet engine. He has all five of these students learning various functions of the engine by hands-on training. (Museum of North Texas.)

Learning Mechanics. US Air Force mechanics worked on both fixed-wing and rotary-wing aircraft at Sheppard Air Force Base. This instructor is explaining the correct lineup of gears and O-rings in the props of a helicopter to students. (Museum of North Texas.)

Memorial Service. This memorial service was held for one of Sheppard Air Force Base's NATO officers who was killed while a student attending pilot training. Comrades are lined up at attention as the wreath and casket are departing from Base Chapel 3. (Museum of North Texas.)

NONCOMMISSIONED OFFICER. This staff sergeant has a pickup truck assigned to him as the noncommissioned officer (NCO) in charge of the base's auto hobby shop. The markings indicate the truck is a 1965 model. He and another sergeant and two airman seem pleased in having their picture taken. (Museum of North Texas.)

Deadly Tuesday, Part One. On April 3, 1964, a death-dealing tornado ripped through Sheppard Air Force Base, destroying two civilian housing developments and a trailer park. In all, seven military personnel and 23 dependents were injured. In Wichita Falls, seven persons were killed and over 60 injured. At the base, two KC-97 tankers belonging to Strategic Air Command (SAC) received damage. The tornado missed a new $5 million hospital at Sheppard. (Museum of North Texas.)

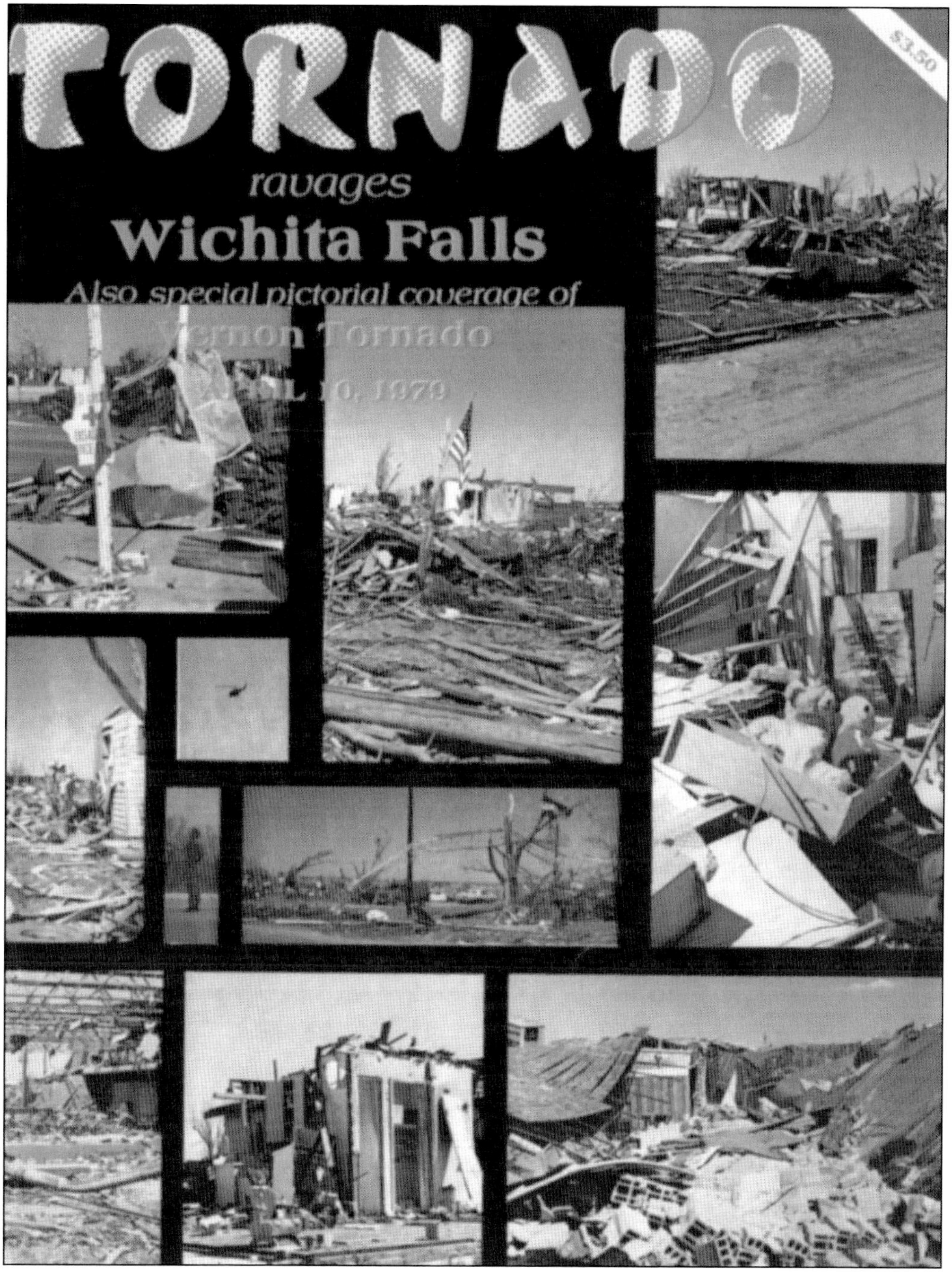

Deadly Tuesday, Part Two. Fifteen years later, on April 10, 1979, another tornado barely missed the base but took a huge toll on the city of Wichita Falls, with 44 killed, 1,000 injured, and property damage at $300 million. This tornado is vividly remembered, even today, as Deadly Tuesday. (Museum of North Texas.)

MISS *TEXOMA*, A HELICOPTER. These two unidentified colonels are about to preflight *Miss Texoma*, a helicopter assigned to Sheppard Air Force Base in 1963. (Museum of North Texas.)

Miss Texoma. Above is another view of the helicopter, *Miss Texoma*. Sheppard Air Force Base trained both fixed- and rotary-wing pilots. (Museum of North Texas.)

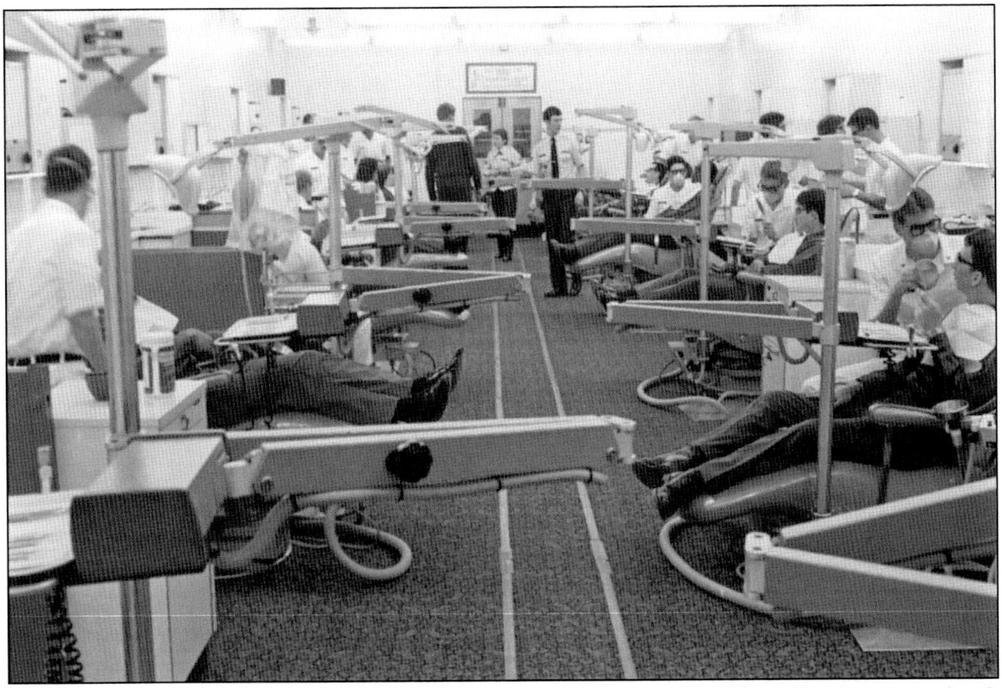

Dental Technician School. Sheppard Air Force Base has a large dental technician school, training technicians Air Force wide. Students did not practice on the populace but upon each other. (Museum of North Texas.)

Main Gate Display. As times change, the US Air Force changes displays to coincide with modernization. These changes for the main gate's sign have not occurred often, but each new sign looks better and better. (US Air Force.)

Seven

SHEPPARD TODAY

SECURITY FOR MAIN GATE. This base policeman stands at parade rest while directing traffic through the main gate. If a vehicle did not display the appropriate sticker, the driver would be stopped and his or her identity verified from valid identification cards. Nonmilitary visitors were sent to a building nearby to obtain visitor passes. The policeman is wearing a loaded sidearm, and another policeman is on duty observing those exiting the gate. The gatehouse had a phone is case higher authority needed notification. (Courtesy of the Museum of North Texas.)

ENGINEERING. These civil engineer students are attending courses in the electrical field to learn how to become line repairmen and electricians. (Museum of North Texas.)

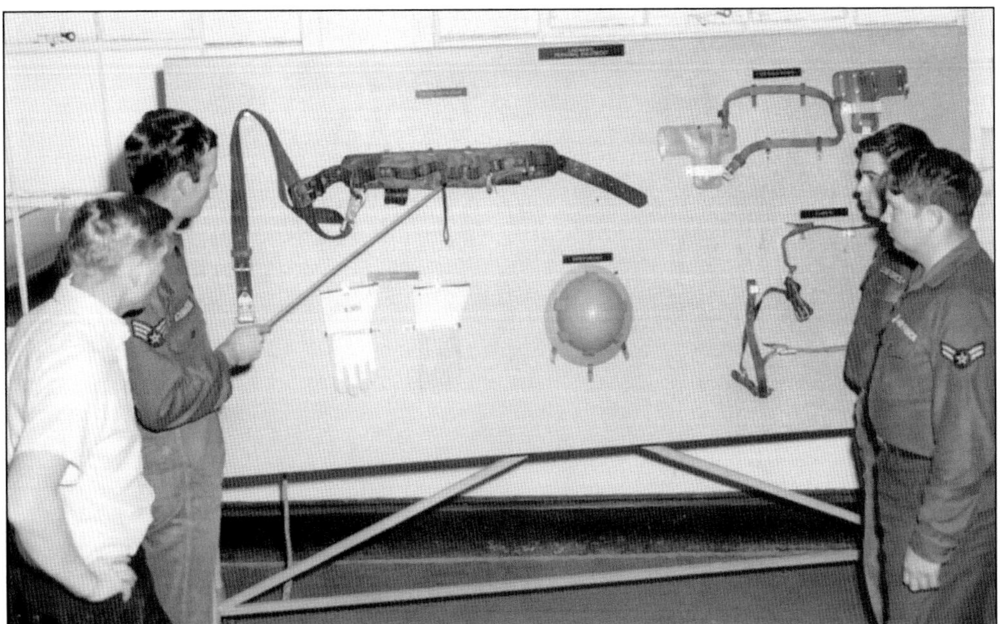

THE PURPOSE OF CLIMBING. Sergeant Correla explores the purpose of climbing equipment to students enrolled in the 3ABR54231 Electric Power Line Specialist Course around 1960. (Museum of North Texas.)

Civil Engineer's Plumbing. These two airmen are students practicing learned skills in the civil engineer's plumbing course at Sheppard Air Force Base. (Museum of North Texas.)

View from Control Tower. This view of the flight line was taken from the control tower. Different kinds of aircraft, including T-38, helicopter, F4, and F-14 Tomcat, are parked on the ramp. (Museum of North Texas.)

Civil Engineer Squadron. These airmen of the Civil Engineer Squadron have deplaned from a C-130 at Sheppard Air Force Base. The airmen have been deployed on temporary duty and have returned to home base. (Museum of North Texas.)

Noncommissioned Officers. This squadron seems to be top heavy with mostly noncommissioned officers in formation at parade rest while they receive a briefing by the commander. The unit commander is the woman standing in the front right. (Museum of North Texas.)

T-38 Falcon in Flight. Pictured is a T-38 Falcon over Sheppard Air Force Base, flown by pilots of the 90th Flying Training Squadron. (US Air Force.)

Weathering the Storm. Pilots were required to fly in all types of weather and conditions, not to mention all the mechanical and natural hazards that may occur. This officer is attending the Officer Course B241-1. The course teaches use of radar as the primary means of navigation. (Museum of North Texas.)

REPAIRING A PROP ENGINE. These students are working on an aircraft's prop engine. The sergeant is the instructor, and the civilian is a technical representative from the aircraft manufacturer on the scene to assistance and insure modifications are carried out according to directives. (Museum of North Texas.)

T-37B Tweet Trainer. Most of the T-37B Tweet trainer aircraft was removed from Sheppard and the Air Force inventory; this one made it to the National Museum of the Air Force to be maintained and displayed and to become an Air Force relic in time. (US Air Force.)

Instructor and Student. The instructor pilot and student are preparing to taxi for takeoff in this T-38 Falcon jet trainer. They are about to close the canopy and fly a sortie. (Museum of North Texas.)

Taking a Break. These medical officers are taking a break from training to partake the noon meal at the base hospital mess hall. A squadron commander or first sergeant would frown and likely correct three of the officers with hands in their pockets unless they were reaching for change. (Museum of North Texas.)

Teaching Future Pilots. Technical Sergeant Roberts explains the functionality of an air intake valve to his students as they study all the functions of a vehicle's engine. (Museum of North Texas.)

Visit from the Vice President. Then–vice president George H.W. Bush visits Sheppard Air Force Base in 1983. The space shuttle *Challenger* returned to Kennedy Space Center via Sheppard Air Force Base. (Museum of North Texas.)

Memorial Day Parade. The 82nd Training Wing at Sheppard Air Force Base participates in the Memorial Day Parade, and these troops are displaying the flags of states and military branches. (US Air Force.)

C-130 Lockheed Spectre. The C-130 Lockheed Spectre has been used extensively all over the world by the US Air Force. It hauls cargo, troops, and even sprays chemicals defoliants. (US Air Force.)

Pilot's View. This is a pilot's view of the controls inside the cockpit of the C-130 Lockheed Spectre. The instrumentation would be mind-boggling to the novice. (US Air Force.)

B-52H Bomber. This B-52H has landed at Sheppard Air Force Base to be assigned as a trainer. The flight-line security personnel are setting up a perimeter to safeguard and prevent unauthorized entry. (US Air Force.)

Old Training Aircraft. These T-37B Tweet trainer aircraft, last of 74 in the inventory, depart from Sheppard Air Force Base. The trainers were phased out and replaced by the new T-6A Texan

II trainers. (US Air Force.)

Repair and Maintenance. This is another view of the huge B-52H heavy bomber that had just arrived at Sheppard Air Force Base for training purposes. Students will learn all aspects of repair and maintenance for the B-52H. (US Air Force.)

T-6A Texan II Trainer. The T-6A Texan II trainer replaced the T-37Bs. Col. David Peterson (left), 80th Flight Training wing commander, and Royal Netherlands Air Force air commodore Peter Berlijn (right) are doing a preflight on one of the 69 new T-6As, which replaced the 74 T-37 Tweets. (US Air Force.)

Preparing for Takeoff. 1st Lt. Stephen Thomas (left) and Capt. Lars Holten of Norway are preparing for takeoff in a T-38 Talon at Sheppard Air Force Base. (US Air Force.)

RAPID INTERVENTION VEHICLE. This new Rapid Intervention Vehicle (RIV) is the newest addition to the crash response fleet. The bumper-mounted hose turret is being operated by firefighter Carl Lamb. (US Air Force.)

WALKING TO CLASS. These enlisted airmen are marching to class. They are housed in barracks that has its own orderly room, day room, laundry, dining hall, and student rooms. The reflective safety gear is worn to give the marching students protection during darkness or dim lighting. (US Air Force.)

Helicopter. This Air Force officer has taken the controls of the helicopter in preparation for a flight as the copilot seems to be cleaning the windshield with a cloth. The writing stenciled beside the pilot seat reads, "CREWCHIEF A1C RD MILLER." (Museum of North Texas.)

Training Time. Officer instructor Payne is taking an unidentified NATO student pilot up for another few hours of training. (Museum of North Texas.)

First Solo Flight. 2nd Lt. Brittany Dippel of the 80th Flight Training Wing's EURO-NATO joint jet pilot training has completed her first solo flight in the T-6A Texan II trainer on February 25, 2015. When a student pilot completes his or her first solo flight, he or she gets a dunking. (US Air Force.)

Repairing Damaged Aircraft. The 362nd Training Squadron is using heavy equipment to recover a damaged aircraft. The terminology for the procedure is Crash Damaged Disabled Aircraft Recovery (CDDAR), and these students are training with the recovery of a F-15 Eagle. The plane's landing gear failed upon landing on October 28, 2013. (US Air Force.)

JN-4 CURTISS JENNY TRAINER. From Jennys to jets brings forth the 1917 JN-4 Curtiss Jenny trainer at Call Field. World War II and Korean War veteran pilot Tom Dunaher is at the controls during a 2009 Air Show at Sheppard Air Force Base. (Museum of North Texas.)

FLIGHT AT SUNRISE. The Jenny is followed into the present with this T-38 Talon jet as the pilot takes off at sunrise at Sheppard Air Force Base. Today's Air Force continues its role at Sheppard Air Force Base as the world leader in military training. (Museum of North Texas.)

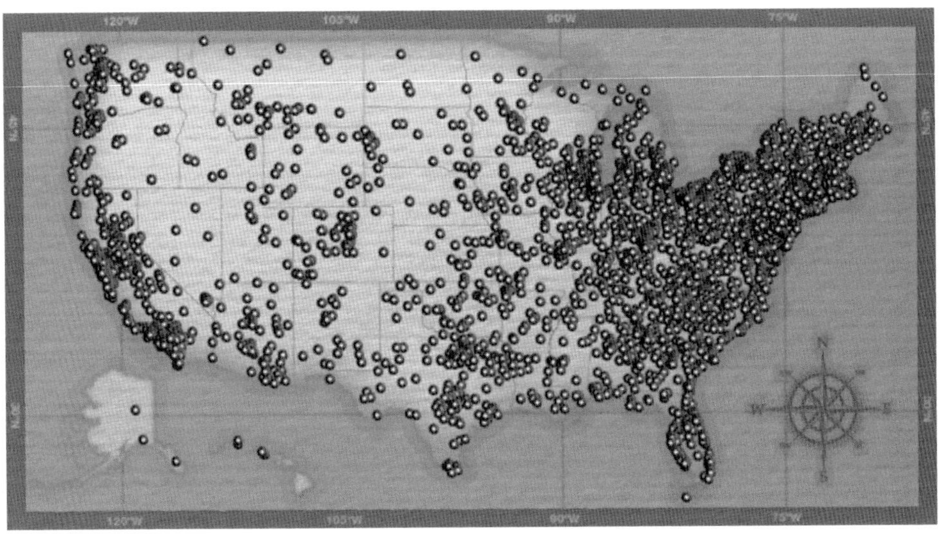